A UNIQUE AND IDENTICAL ENGLISH GRAMMAR & COMPOSITION

Chinmoy Dutta

A UNIQUE AND IDENTICAL ENGLISH GRAMMAR & COMPOSITION

By

Chinmoy Dutta

Copyright© Chinmoy Dutta 2022

Originally published in India

Edition: 1

ISBN: 978-93-91041-24-3

Published by RIGI PUBLICATION

777, Street no.9, Krishna Nagar Khanna-141401 (Punjab), India

Website: www.rigipublication.com

Email: info@rigipublication.com

Phone: +91-9357710014, +91-9465468291

PREFACE

This book serves as will be seen, the purpose of the students preparing for the class IX & X under the guidelines of New syllabus. All the sections under this syllabus. Writing skills, Grammar and vocabulary have been dealt with in detail with copious examples and exercises to help the students to practice. The teacher will also find this volume especially helpful in the classroom as the exercises provide the students with materials to write on and space to write in. I have spared no pains to make this book helpful and attractive to stimulate the interest of the students.

Author
Chinmoy Dutta.
MA.in English.

A UNIQUE AND IDENTICAL
ENGLISH GRAMMAR &
COMPOSITION

TABLE OF CONTENTS

TENSES

PRESENT TENSE

Present Indefinite.

Present Continuous.

Present Perfect

Present Perfect Continuous.

PAST TENSE

Past Indefinite

Past Continuous

Past Perfect

Past Perfect Continuous.

FUTURE TENSE

Future Indefinite.

Future Continuous

Future Perfect

Future Perfect Continuous.

Present Tense

Present Indefinite

1.   This form is used in case of

Things happening in the present

Example... He is a student.

2.   Something that happens repeatedly

Example.. He helps his father.

3.   A habit or a routine

Example... He goes to school.

4. To make future time reference when the event is part of a fixed time table.

Example... This year Janmashtami falls on Sunday.

5. In exclamatory sentences...

Example... Here comes the bus!

6. In commentaries

Example... Raju runs forward and takes a catch.

7. Instead of present continuous with certain verbs

Example... I see smoke. /I have a pen.

The following table shows the different forms of the present indefinite tense.

Affirmative Sentences.

He/She/It +1stform of the verb +s/es.

Example.. He/She/It eats apples.

I/We/You/They+1stform of the verb +object

Example... I/we/You/They eat apples.

Negative Sentences.

He/She/It does not+Ist form of the verb +object.

Example..He/She/It doesn't play cricket.

I/We/You/they+1stform of the verb +object

Present Continuous

Usage The present continuous

1. To refer to something happening at the time of speaking.

Example.. Please don't talk so loudly. I am studying.

2. When we talk about something connected with the present time.

Example.. These days more and more people are learning a foreign language

3. When we refer to a situation that is more or less temporary

Example... She is looking for her spectacles.

4. For an action that is planned for the near future.

Example....I am going to see a movie today.

5. For a persistent habit

Example... My dog is rather silly, She is always looking out for an opportunity to gorge the dustbin.

T3 Present Continuous is formed with the present tense of the auxiliary 'be'+the present participle.

Fill in the blanks with the correct form of the verbs given in brackets.

1. The CAS (make)a lot of money these days.

2. Why (be) he (not help) You. ?

3. (be)You (come)to my house today?

4. The band (play)all the old songs.

5. His parents (visit)him today evening.

6. Vijay (behave) very foolishly.

7. By ignoring the traffic signal, they (break)the law.

8. It (rain)heavily outside.

9. Our cook (no come)today.

10. We(face) a lot of problems in our society these days.

11. The driver (plan)to take off tomorrow.

12. I (come) to the party to night.

13. The children(play)hide and seek in the garden..

14. The train (run)late.

15. Today, the sun (shine)bright.

16. Farmers(plucking)berries from the bushes.

Present Perfect

Usage. The present perfect tense is used to or completed in the immediate past.

1. To indicate activities completed in the immediate past.

Example.. He has just gone out.

2. To Express past actions when no definite time is given.

Example... I have read Gulliver travels.

3. To describe past events that have an impact on the present.

Example... He has eaten up all the biscuits.

I have cut my finger.

4. To denote an action that began in the past but continues up to today.

(Using for, since, etc.)

Example... I have known him since 1990.

Words often used with the present perfect tense. 'Yet', ' 'sofor', 'never', 'ever', 'already', 'since', 'just now', 'several times'.

Affirmative Sentences.

Subject +has/have+3rd form of the verb+object…

Present Perfect Continuous.

This form is used to refer to something that began in the past but is still happening at the time of speaking

Example… I have been reading Gulliver's travels for the last week.

Words often used with the present perfect continuous tense.

Since/For

Since.. suggest the point of time for suggests the period of time.

Affirmative Sentences.

Subject +Has/have +1st form of the verb +since/for +time.

Example.. Your father has been looking for you for two hours.

They have been looking for you for two hours.

Negative Sentences.

Subject +has/have +not +been +1st form of the verb +ing+since/for +time.

Example....The gardener has not been watering the plants for two hours.

Past Indefinite.

Usage. The simple past (past indefinite tense)is used to.

1. An action completed in the past

Example....He left for Delhi yesterday.

2. A past habit or a routine

Example... He went to school by bus but now he walks.

3. Words often used with the past indefinite tense.

Yesterday, ago, last.

Affirmative Sentences.

Subject +2nd form of the verb +object.

Example....Roshan completed his work yesterday.

Negative Sentences.

Subject +did not +1st form of the verb +object.

Example.. He did not complete his work yesterday.

Interrogative Sentences.

Did +subject +1st form of the verb +object+?

Example... Did your father scold you for your mistake?

Wh.. family+did +subject+1st form of the verb +object?

Example.. Why did your father scold you.

Past Continuous

Usage. The past continuous tense is used to

1. To refer to something happening at the time of reference in the past

Example... We're eating our dinner when he came.

2. When we talk about something that was a persistent habit in the past

Example... He was always grumbling.

Affirmative Sentences.

Subject +was/were +1st form of the verb +ing+object

Example... He was watching a film.

They were watching a film.

Negative Sentences.

Subject +was/were+1st form of the verb +ing+object

Example...He was not watching a film.

They were not watching a film.

Interrogative Sentences

Was/were +subject +1st form of the verb +ing+object +?

Example... Was he playing cricket in the field?

Wh... family +was/were+subject +1st form of the verb

Past Perfect.

This form is used to indicate the earlier of the two activities that happened in the past.

Example....The train had already left by the time I reached the station.

Affirmative Sentences.

Subject+had+3rd form of the verb+object.

Example... He had taken his breakfast when the mother arrived.

Negative Sentences.

Subject +hadn't +3rd form of the verb +object

Example..... He hadn't taken his breakfast when the mother arrived.

Interrogative Sentences.

Had+subject+3rd form of the verb +object +?

Example....Had he gone to the theatre?

Why..family+had+subject+3rd form of the verb +object +?

Example....why had the driver locked the car?

Fill in the blanks with the correct form of the verbs given in ...

Past Perfect Continuous.

This form is used to refer to something begun in the past and continued up to a point of reference in the past.

Example....I had been reading Gulliver's travels for the last week when he came to see me.

Affirmative Sentences.

Subject+had been+1st form of the verb+ing+object+since+for+time

Example... I had been waiting for my friend for 3 hours.

Negative Sentences.

Subject+hadn't been+1st form of the verb+ing+object+since+for+time.

Example....I hadn't been waiting for my friend for 3 hours.

Interrogative Sentences.

Had+subject+been+1st form of the verb+ing+object+since for+time?

Example... Had you been cleaning the place since morning?

Wh..family+had+subject+been+1st form of the verb+ing+object

Future Indefinite

Usage. The future indefinite tense an action that will take place in the future.

Example....I shall see you shortly.

He will bring the book.

1. The future indefinite is also used to Express the speakers opinion or assumption about the future.

a.Now that the book is in the market, the sales will go up.

b. to Express habitual actions which are likely to take place.

Example… The sky is over cast, it will rain today.

c. to Express announcements of future plans and weather forecasts.

Example.. The flood waters will continue to recede how words often used with the future indefinite tense.

Affirmative Sentences.

Subject +will/shall +1st form of the verb +object

Example... He will arrive.

Future Continuous

Usage. The future continuous tense like the other continuous tense is used with a point of time. It expresses an action that will be going on at the time of speaking.

Example... Puja will be reading a book at that time.

Affirmative Sentences

Subject +will/shall +be-1st form of the verb +ing+object.

Example... You shall be giving the lecture to night.

Negative Sentences

Subject +will/shall or, not+be+1st form of the verb +ing+object

Example... He will not be giving the lecture to night.

Interrogative Sentences.

Will/shall +subject +1st form of the verb +ing+object +?

Example... Will they be playing in the ground in that heat?

Why family +Will/shall +subject +be +1st form of the verb +ing+object +?

Future Perfect Continuous

Usage. The future perfect continuous tense denotes an action that will be finished at some definite time in the future, but which had been going on before it was finished.

Example.. He will have been watching the show at the 'kingdom of dreams 'tomorrow night.

Affirmative Sentences.

Subject +will/shall +have been +1st form of the verb +ing+object

Example.. You will have been celebrating your birthday tomorrow this time.

Negative Sentences.

Subject +will/shall not +have been +1st form of the verb +ing+object

Example... The programme will not have been going on without the manager's consent.

Interrogative Sentences.

Will/shall +subject +have been +1st form of the verb +ing+object +?

Exercise

Fill in the blanks with the correct form of the verbs given in brackets.

Question No 1

Once when I (a).................(cross)the road. (b)............................(see)a small boy who(c).................... (look)quite lost. (d)......................(ask) him the name of his parents but he(e)................ (can)not answer. After waiting for a little while, I (f).................(bring) him home and (g)....................... (feed) him.

(Answer)

a. Was crossing

b. Saw

c. Looked

d. Asked

e. Could

f. Brought

g. Fed

Question No 2

(a) I..................... (feel) very sorry to see the pathetic condition of the slums. (b). children........................ (be)shabbily dressed and were running all over the place. A small girl (c)............... (eat) banana. She (d)..................... (get) it from her father. Her father (e)...................(be) a poor labourer. Her mother always (f)....................(remain) sick.

(Answer)

a. Felt

b. Were

c. Was eating

d. Had got

e. Was

f. Remained

Question No 3

As per the prediction of the met. Department it (a).................... (rain) tomorrow. On hearing this, the farmer (b).................... (start) dancing. There (c).................... (be) no rain in their area for a long time. This weather prediction (d).................... (make) everybody happy.

(Answer)

a. Will rain

b. Started

c. Had been

d. Made

Question No 4

Seema, my classmate is (a)................. (celebrate) her birthday tomorrow. I (b).................... (want) to gift her a science puzzle but (c)................... (not know) where to buy it from I (d)...................
(will/shall) ask my father in the evening when he (e)................... (return) home from work.

(Answer)

a. Celebrating

b. Want

c. Do not know

d. Shall

e. Returns

Question No 5

It's a bright afternoon. The sun (a)................... (shine) in the sky. The children's (b)................... (play) in the garden where there (c)................... (be) lots of plants. squirrels (d)................... (nibble) at the small piece of food. The place (e)................... (be) buzzing with activity. We (f)................... (be) all very happy and enjoying the place.

(Answer)

a. Is shining

b. Are playing

c. Are

d. Are nibbling

e. Is

f. Are

Question No 6

Two children (a)..................... (be) playing in the backyard of their house when they (b)..................... (spot) a tiger cub. Mistaking it for a big cat, they (c)..................... (bring) it home and (d)..................... (hide) it. When their parents (e)..................... (comeback) that they (f)..................... (decide) that they (g)..................... (Will/Shall) not disclose the presence of the big cat to their parents.

(Answer)

a. Were

b. Spotted

c. Brought

d. Hid

e. Came back

f. Decided

g. Would

Question No 7

Fill in the blanks with the correct form the verbs given in brackets.

The students (a)..................... (organise) a rally to bring awareness among the locals regarding pollution. Many junior students also (b)..................... (join)it-They (c).....................(stage)a street play which (d)..................... (appreciate)by one and all. All the activities (e).....................(be)very successful. These (f).....................(be aim)to bring about awareness among people.

(Answer)

a. Have organised./Organised.

b. Joined.

c. Staged

d. Was appreciated

e. Were

f. Were aimed.

Question No 8

Weall (a).................... (need)changes it (be).......................(refresh)and (c).................... (relax)our minds schools and colleges too give long holidays to students to (d)................... (rejuvenate) themselves, Holidays (e)................... (be) a welcome change. In our country, We (f).................. (be) number of holidays on account of religious and national festivals.

(Answer)

a. Need

b. Refreshes

c. Relaxes

d. Rejuvenate

e. Are

f. Have

Question No 9

Fill in the blanks with the correct form of the verbs given in brackets.

An old couple(a).................... (cross)the road when a speeding truck (b)....................(hit)them from behind. The old man (c)..................(fly)into the air while the woman (d)................(lie)bleeding on the ground. People (e)................... (gather)and (f).................(take)them to the hospital where they (be)................... (declare)brought.

(Answer)

1. Was crossing

2. Hit

3. Was flying.

4. Was lying

5. gathered

6. Took

7. Were declared.

Question No 10

Romila (a)...................... (go)to a hotel to celebrate her birth day in the evening. Many guests (b)................(invite). Her father (c)............(buy)a new dress for her and the mother. (d)..................(order)a chocolate cake. Today she (e)................. (turn) sixteen. She remembers that last year. She (f)................ (gift) a bicycle by her parents.

(Answer)

a. Went

b. Were invited

C. Bought

d. Ordered

e. Turns/turned

f. Was gifted

Question no 11.

Fill in the blanks with the correct form of the verbs given in brackets.

What (a)...................(do)you do if there(b)................... (be)no body to receive you at the railway station? (c)................... (will/shall)you take a cab on your own or (d)................ (will/shall)you wait there? you(e)................ (not carry)much luggage but the one bag that you (f)...................(be) is quite heavy.

(Answer)

a. Do

b. Is

c. Will

d. Will

e. Are not carrying

f. Have

Question no 12.

Fill in the blanks with the correct form of the verbs given in brackets.

Rosy(a)...........(fell)sick so her mother (b)................(take)her to a nearby doctor The doctor said, "you (c)..................(must)take the medicine regularly and (d).................(drive) lots of build". Rosy(e).................(not play)much attention to the doctor's words which (f)................. (make) him scold her.

Answer:

a. Had fallen

b. Took

c. Must

d. Drink

e. Did not play

f. Made

MODALS

What are the Modal Verbs?

Modals (also called modal verbs, modal auxiliary verbs, modal auxiliaries are special verbs which behave irregularly in English. They are different from normal verbs like "work, play, visit "They give additional information about the function of the main verb that follows it They have a great variety of communicative functions.

Modals are verbs used to Express the mood or attitude of the speaker. They are used before ordinary verbs and express meanings such as permission, possibility, certainly and necessity. Modals haven't s/es in the third person singular. They have no infinitive and ing form.

Has to/Have to

(a)'Has to ' and 'Have to 'are used to Express some compulsion, necessity obligation in the present or future tenses. The expression 'had to' is the past tense of 'has to' and 'have to' and serves the same function.

Rajendra has to finish his work on time.

I have to withdraw money from the bank.

He had to move the Almira himself.

(b) In negative and questions, 'Have to' and 'had to' are used with 'do' 'does' and 'did'.

They don't have to worry about food.

She doesn't have to finish the drawings.

Prem didi ji have to go.

She (Mustn't)go late for the interview.

Should/Shouldn't

1. "should" is used in all persons to express duty or obligation.

We (should) obey the laws.

You (should)be honest.

Children (shouldn't)deface the walls.

She (should)respect her elder brother.

2. "Should" is used to Express caution or purpose

Work hard lest you (should)fail.

Walk carefully lest you (should)fall.

3. Advice

You (should)not speak loudly.

She (should)learn the facts properly.

We(should)not jump to conclusions.

4. Guess/supposition

It (shouldn't) rain. The sky is clear

If my father (should)see me at the restaurant, he will be annoyed.

The baby (should)be about a year old.

It(shouldn't)take them more than three hours to reach here.

5. Need

"Need" is used to express necessity or obligation generally in an interrogative sentence in the present tense.

Need. You worry about your last documents.

Need: I tell you more?

Need: She pay the amount?

Needn't/Need not

Needn't/Need not is used to express necessity in the negative sense.

I need not meet him.

I can very well hear you. You needn't shout.

You need not have abused him.

6. Must

Must doesn't have a past tense form. We can use 'must' to talk about the present or the future. To talk about the past we I see had to (The past from of 'have to') Must is used to express…

(a)Compulsion

You must see the doctor at once.

He must work hard in order to pass.

(b)Duty

One must serve one's country.

We must respect our parents.

(c)Obligation

You must help our neighbours.

One must obey one's elders.

(d)Necessity

If you want to reach on time, You must run fast.

You must speak loudly if you want to be heard.

(e) Logical Certainly

It is getting dark. She must have left already living in such abnormal conditions must be difficult.

Mustn't

Mustn't is used to convey the sense of obligation compulsion etc. as in the case of must but in the negative sense.

We Mustn't waste our time.

You have fever. You Mustn't jump around.

She Mustn't go late for the interview.

7. Ought to

We use ought to when talking about things which are desired or ideal. You use ought to have with a past participle to indicate that something was expected to happen or be the case, but it did not happen or was not the case.

1. Obligation or Desirability.

We ought to love our neighbours.

You ought to respect your elders.

He ought to get the promotion.

2. Duty

We ought to help the poor.

You ought to respect the traffic rules.

3. Probability

The price of onions ought to come down soon.

4. Logical deduction

The book has been received well it ought to fetch.

Exercise.

Use "should/must/ought to" appropriately in the following sentences.

1. The students...................respect their teacher

2 Every student............. carry his or her I card during the examination.

2. You...................keep away from bad habits like teasing girls, copying in exam etc.

4. Madhu seems to be quite exhausted she...................take some rest.

5. What are you doing these days. It is a wild goose chase. you................... rather. Concentrate on your own project.

6. Sejal has searched the file everywhere, but didn't find it. I think it....................be in the Almira at the drawing room.

7. Many new investors have started popping up these days. The stock exchange rates................... go on rising in coming few days.

Answers: 1. Ought to(Moral Obligation), 2. Must (compulsion),   3. Should 4. Should (suggestions), 5. Should (suggestions), 6. Must (Possibility), 7. Ought to (Moral Obligation)

Pick out the correct sentences from among the four sentences in each of the following.

1. a. I was able to pass the exam. But I couldn't appear for it.

b. I could pass the exam. But I did not appear for it.

C. I was able to pass the exam. But I did not appear ed for it.

d. I was able to pass the exam but I did not appear for it.

2. a. Nobody knows his where abouts. He may be there in Doha.

b. Nobody knows his where abouts. He is there in Doha.

c. Nobody knows his where abouts. He might be there in Doha.

d. Nobody knows his where abouts. He should be there in Doha.

3. a. The drug addicts may not be tortured but should be rehabilitated.

b. The drug addicts cannot be tortured but must be rehabilitated.

c. The drug addicts should not be tortured but might be rehabilitated.

d. The drug addicts must not be tortured but should be rehabilitated.

4. (a)you ought to help the blind to cross the road.

(b)you must help the blind to cross the road.

c. you ought to help the blind to crossing the road.

d. you should to help the blind to crossing the road.

2. you should help the blinds to cross the road.

5. (a)you need not worry at all. I am take care of your luggage.

(b)you Needn't worry at all. I will take care of your luggage.

c. you need to not worry at all. I will taking care of your luggage

d. you need not worry at all. I will be take care of your luggage.

6. (a) Everyone should follow the path. shown by his or her parents and teachers.

(b)Every one may be follow the path shown by their parents and teachers

c. Everyone should be follow the path shown by his or her parents and teachers.

d. Everyone might follow the path shown by his or her parents and teachers.

7. a) Abhi can achieve his goal if they have strong determination.

b). Abhi may achieve his goal if he had strong determination.

c. Abhi can achieve his goal but he has strong determination.

d. Abhi can achieve his goal if he has strong determination.

8. a)This seems to be difficult. but I will make this happen.

b. This seem to be difficult. But I may make this happen.

c. This seems to be difficult. But I shall make this happen.

d. This seemed to be difficult but I should make this happen.

9. a)one should not too careful about what is good or what is bad?

b)one should not be too careful about what is good or what is bad?

c. one may not be too careful about what is good or what is bad?

d. one will not be too careful about what is good or what is bad?

10. a)He might be pass the exam in the first attempt.

b)He must be pass the exam in the first attempt.

c) He must pass the exam in the first attempt.

d) He should be pass the exam in the first attempt.

Answer: 1. b, 2. d, 3. d, 4. a, 5. b, 6. a, 7. d, 8. a, 9. b, 10. c

PREPOSITIONS

A preposition is a word placed before.

A noun or pronoun to show the relation between the noun or pronoun to some other word in a sentence.

1. A preposition may join in a

1. Noun to another noun g. There is a pen in my bag.

2. Noun to an adjective. g. They are found of ice cream.

3. Noun to verb g she shouted for help.

2. The same preposition can be used to show a relationship with time, space, Rate, State and Direction.

1. I'll come at 5 o'clock. (time)

1. She is sitting at the window. (space)

3. Mangoes sell at Rs. 50 per kg. (rate)

4. The cricketers are at a loss. (state)

5. The girls rushed at the film star. (Direction).

(Preposition of time)

Time has two dimension:

a)paint of time

b)period of time.

3. At- At is used point of time...

Himachal Pradesh is very beautiful in winters.

We are living in the twenty first century

Before morning/afternoon/evening. meet me in the evening.

He goes to school in the evening.

Before a period of time.

You have to finish this work in a week.

I shall be back in an hour.

4. After-To indicate following in time or later then.

Don't go out after dark.

The doctor came after the death of the patient.

Meet me at my office after lunch.

I 'm leaving for Mumbai the day after tomorrow.

5. Before-To indicate 'earlier then'.

Come back before dark.

The patient had died before the doctor came.

Meet me before dinner. I went there the day before yesterday.

6. By-To indicate the meaning of 'not later than or as soon as'

I shall finish the syllabus by January.

It will be dark by the time you reach home. By 25th January I shall have finished your course.

They decided to end up the party by midnight.

7. During

To indicate the meaning of 'throughout the continuance of '

The sun gives us light during the day.

During my college days I watched many movies.

What did he do during my absence?

James slept during his lesson.

8. For... To indicate extent of time.

We are leaving for Delhi for a week.

My uncle is going abroad for a month.

To indicate period of time in the perfect tenses.

They have been playing for four hours.

It has been raining for two days.

9. Since

To indicate a point of time.

I Have been Studying since 5 p.m.

It has been raining since morning.

10. Through-To indicate 'From 'beginning to end of time.'

You can't work through the day in summer. It is very hot.

Student can't sit quietly through a boring lesson.

11. Till /until -To indicate 'up to the time when 'or 'not earlier then'

Until his marriage he spent the time with his friends.

A labour works hard from morning till night.

12. With in-To indicate 'innless then time 'you should complete your examination papers within the stipulated time.

I'll come back from Mumbai within a week.

13. with-To indicate 'at same time as 'with the approach of the clouds it becomes dark.

We must rise with the sun.

14. From-To indicate the starting of a period of time.

Our examinations will start from 10th march.

I'll join office from Monday.

15. Between -used when two times are mentioned.

The director will be arriving any time between 3 and 4 o'clock.

Preposition of place /space.

1. At-To indicate the place in which somebody or something is/was/will be.

I shall meet you at the station.

In the evening Sahil was at his brother's house.

The soldiers rushed at the enemy.

The airport is at a distance from the city

2. In-To indicate position or something in a surrounded place.

Kangaroo is found in Australia.

The culprits are standing in the corner of the court room.

Mary has gone in the direction.

The soldier was wounded in the leg.

3. On-To indicate the position of a thing covering or forming part of a surface that is at rest.

Leaves are floating on the water.

4. Across-To indicate 'from side to side'

There are many bridges across the Ganga.

Can you ferry me across the river? Draw a lion the sheet of paper.

5. Before-To indicate the meaning of 'in front of '.

The accused was brought before the judge

Jackson is standing before Philips in the queue for the movie ticket.

6. In front of-To indicate the meaning of 'directly before'

There are some mango trees in front of my uncle's house.

There is a fountain in front of C.A.D. circle.

7. Above-To indicate 'higher then 'or' at higher point'.

The sun rose above the horizon.

The flood water came above our knees.

The kite is flying above the clouds.

8. Over-To indicate a thing covering the surface party or completely.

The waiter spread a table cloth over the table.

9. Under -To -To indicate a position lower then 'for both persons and things.

The cat is under the table.

I sat under the tree.

10. Under Neath-It is used for thing only.

The shoes are kept underneath the table.

11. Among-used with more than two persons or things.

He divided his property among his four sons.

The village is situated among the hills.

The teacher distributed the sweets among his students.

1. Beside

2. It means 'by the side of '.

The child is playing beside his mother.

His house is beside his hospital.

1. Besides.

2. it means 'in addition to'

Besides his job, he also takes private tuitions.

He also has a bungalow in Delhi besides a sea facing flat in Mumbai.

Exercise

Complete the following sentences using appropriate prepositions.

1. Regular exercise is beneficial....................health.

2. He is bent..................... mischief.

3. We must be grateful for the blessings God has bestowed.....................us.

4. He is a hypocrite. Beware....................him.

5. She boasts.............her achievements.

6. The indulgent mother is blind............. her son's fault.

7. He was born.....................poor parents.

8. The ship is bound............... California.

9. The robbers broke..................the shop at midnight and looked it.

10. Emperor Akbar brought................... many social reforms.

11. They brought..........the child tenderly.

(Answer)

1. To

2. On

3. On

4. Of

5. Of

6. To

7. Of/To

8. For

9. Into

10. About

11. Up

Fill in the blanks with suitable prepositions.

1. The Rajdhani Express departs....................3pm...................... Mumbai.

2. Human sacrifices were practiced..................some of the tribes living in this area.

3. I received his message.............6'o clock........................the morning.

4. ....last month I have seen him but once.

5. ....rice they had curry.

6. His fever has taken a turn for the better......................yesterday.

7. She has spent all her life.................... Hyderabad.

8. I saw him felling a big tree...............just a hatchet.

(Answer)

1. At, From 2. By 3. At, In 4. Since 5. Besides 6. Since 7. In 8. With

DETERMINER

1. 'Determiner' is a word used before a noun to indicate which things or people we are talking about. The words a, the, my, this, some, many, etc., are called determiners

He is a good boy.

The boy you met is my friend.

This novel is very interesting.

I have some information about the accident.

There were many people at the station.

2. Kinds of determiners.

1. Pre Determiners-all, all of, half, half of, both, double, twice, quite, rather, such, what, etc.

Articles-a, an, the.

Demonstrative-this, these, that, those

Possessives-My, our, your, his, her, its, their.

Ordinals-first, second, next, last etc.

Cardinals or numerals-one, two, three, ten, hundred, thousand etc.

Quantifiers-much, some, no, any, many, enough, several, lot of, plenty of, little, few, all, both, another

2. we use the definite article to refer to specific persons or things.

I want to meet the principal in the school.

The tourists crossed the river in a boat.

3. The definite article is used to refer to the things that are only one in the world.

The moon and stars were shining in the sky.

The sun sets in the west.

The earth revolves round the sun.

4. we use the definite article with the words such as school, university, prison, when we are referring to a particular building. They will visit the school on Monday.

I met him in the university.

5. The definite article may be used with the countable nouns that are used in the singular to refer to things more general.

If you break the law, you will be punished.

He played the violin for half an hour.

6. The definite article is used with time expressions.

I met her in the evening.

She came here in the morning.

7. We use the definite article before something that has already been mentioned.

I met a man at the station.

The man belonged to Tamil Nadu.

8. The definite article is used before a noun that is followed by a relative clause or a prepositional phrase.

The man I met at the station belonged to Haryana.

He put the sweater on the table.

9. The definite article is used to refer to familiar things we use regularly.

She looked at the ceiling.

Suddenly the lights went out.

10. The definite article is used before dates or periods of time.

We met on the 15th of October.

It is a popular music of the 1940.

11. The definite article is used before the names of seas, rivers, deserts, mountains.

The ship crossed the Pacific Ocean.

Delhi stands on the bank of the Yamuna.

The Sahara is a famous desert.

They came across the Himalayas.

12. The definite article is used before the names of large public buildings.

They visited the Taj Mahal.

They went to the town hall.

13. The definite article is used before the superlative adjectives.

He is the best boy in the class.

She is the most beautiful girl in the school.

14. The definite article is used before adjectives such as rich, poor, deaf, dumb, bird, to use them as nouns.

The rich and the poor went to the fair.

We should help the blind.

1. The article 'a' is used before the words which begin with consonant sounds and 'an' is used before the words beginning with vowel sounds. However, some words start with a vowel letter but begin with a consonant sound. so we use the article 'a' before these words

He is a European

This is a unique idea.

There is a one parent family.

He is teaching at a university.

2. We use an before words begin with a vowel sound.

The girl bought an orange.

He is an Indian.

He had an umbrella in his hand.

3. Some words begin with a silent so we use an before them.

He is an honest man.

He is an heir to the throne.

I met him an hour ago.

4. We use 'a' or 'an' before singular countable nouns.

Kolkata is a big city.

The dog is an animal.

5. We use 'a' or 'an' before the names of occupations and professions.

His father is an engineer.

He is a pilot.

6. When we use 'a' before 'little 'and 'few', there is a change in the meaning of these words. 'A few 'is used with plural countable nouns and article with uncountable nouns. 'Few' means not many, while 'a few 'means a small number 'little' means not much, while 'a little 'means some.

Few people visit this temple now.

I know a few students of this school.

There is little water in the bucket.

There is a little milk in the bottle.

7. We use 'a', 'an' before an adjective in a noun phrase.

She is a good girl.

She told me an interesting story.

8. We use 'an' with abbreviations beginning with the following letters.

A, E, F, H, I, L, M, N, O, R, S, X (They should have vowel sounds).

His father is an M. P.

He is an N. R. I.

10. Demonstratives: This, These, That, Those

The demonstrative determiners are used to talk about persons or things that have already been mentioned.

This and These refer to the things that are near and can be seen. That and Those are used to refer to the things that are at a distance but can be seen.

We lived in this house for four years.

She bought these books.

Those boys are very mischievous.

I like this school.

I met her this week.

This and that are used for singular nouns and these and those for plural nouns.

Can you lift that box?

Would you like to buy those books?

These boys have done their work.

I have already met that man.

Possessives: my, our, your, his, her, its, their.

Possessives are used to show possession.

He is my uncle.

Our neighbours is a rich man. Your daughter is beautiful.

11. Ordinals: first, second, next, last etc.

The ordinals show what position something has in a series.

He is the first boy who has joined this school.

I shall meet him the next week.

He is the last man to help you.

12. Cardinals: one, two, three, hundred etc.

Cardinals are ordinary numbers like one, two, three etc. They show how many of something there are.

There were only ten boys in the class.

She lived for eighty years.

He has two daughters.

I met three young men at the station.

He balanced himself on one foot.

13. Quantifiers: much, some, several, a lot of, both, all etc.

The quantifiers refer to the quantity of things or amount of something.

There were some people at the airport.

They had enough guests already.

Plenty of people would like to have your job.

Fill in the blanks.

1. .... stray animals have become.........................big nuisance on city roads.

2. I have neither seen....................... elephant nor........................... camel.

3. The other day, Paresh met.......................European................. Canadian, American and..................... Japanese.

4..................... accident occurred at................... crossing.

5. .... inter school drama competition will be held in...................... auditorium.

6. I had.................... eggs for breakfast.

7. Have you been listening to....................news lately.

8. I have............. something to share.

9. Why weren't you carrying................... umbrella.

10. Prem was born in.............. cultured family.

11. What is................... time by your watch?

12. He is neither................... good husband nor................... good father.

13. Come for...............interview tomorrow.

14. ....English is.....................sweet language.

15. I have not seen.................... water bottle you were carrying. It was a very expensive one.

16. Both teams played wonder fully well. But one with a green flag was............. exception.

17. She cooked up..........................story but it was not....................the first time. She had done it.

18. They missed................ o'clock bus, so to kill............. time, they bought a few magazines.

19. Why weren't you carrying ....umbrella?

20. Prem was born in ....cultured family.

21. What is ....time by your watch?

22. He is neither ....good husband nor ....good father.

23. Come for ....interview tomorrow.

24. ....English is ....sweet language.

25. I have not seen ....water bottle you were carrying. It was a very expensive one.

26. Both teams played wonder fully well. But one with a green flag was .... exception.

27.She cooked up................story but it was not ....the first time she had done it.

28 They missed ....8o,clock bus,now they had to wait for an hour for ....next bus,so to kill................time bought a few magazines.

29. ....police nun who caught................thief is ....sincere and hard working person. He was awarded medal ....for the act of bravery last year.

30................entire political system needs to be changed from................top to bottom.

31.Sachin Tendulkar is................Bradman of India. He used to play ....game of cricket with ease,nobody could match upto.

32.I bought................watch................and wallet as birth day gifts through the watch is working fine................wallet'sleather doesn't seen to be of good quality.

33.She was reading ....book on ....life of mother Teresa who was ....inspiration to all.

34.While going to ....office, yesterday, my sister met ....old lady with ....begging bowl in ....her hand and showsin bad shape too.

35. ....police are on ....look out for ....thief who had not only looked jewelllery but had also taken ....motor bikeof the owner. He shared ....bootywith his friends and left ....city.while making good his escape on................motor cycle, he met with ....accident and landed in ....hospital. Later he was ....caught by................police.

36.I desperately needed................break from work as I used to feel exhausted at ....end of ....day. My parents took me to ....specialist who after examining me, prescribed

................supplements. AFTER................WEEK, I felt baller and tanked ....doctor.

(Answer)

1. the, a, the

2. an, a

3. a, a, an, a

4, an, the

5. an, the

6. x

7. the

8. x

9. an

10. a

11. the

12. a, a

13. an

14. x, a

15. the, a

16. the, the, the, an

17. a, the

18. The, the

19.an

20.a

21.the

22.a,a

23.an

24.a

25.the,a

26.the,the,the, an

27.a,the

28.the,an,the,the,a

29.the,the,a,a,an

30.the

31.the, the,an

32.a,a the,the

33.a,the,an

34.the,an,a,a

35.Thethe,a,the,the,the,the,an,a,the

36.a,the,the,a,a,a,the.

VOICE

Voice is that form of the transitive verb that shows whether the subject of the sentence is the doer of the action or has the action done to it.

For example-'Mohan played football. 'This sentence is said to be in the active voice. Here, Mohan is the subject and he is the doer of the action, i.e., 'played football 'The action of the subject is transferred to the object 'football 'because Mohan has done something to the 'football', The passive voice of this sentence is…

Football was played by Mohan.

Here the subject is 'football' which was 'object' in the active sentence. so here something is done to the subject by something or someone.

Rules for the change of voice:

1. The object of the active sentence becomes the subject of the verb in the passive voice. The preposition 'by' is put before it.

2. The main verb of the active sentence changes into the past participle.

3. The form of the verb to be (am/is/are/was/were/being/been) is placed before the main verb according to the tense.

The auxiliary verb is changed according to the new subject in number and person.

3. Changes in persons.

Active voice

(Subjective case)

I

We

You

He

She

It

They

Passive Voice

(Objective case)

By me

By us

By you

By him

By her

By it

By then.

Change in tenses from active voice to passive voice.

Tense/Aspect

Simple present

Simple past

Simple future

Present progressive

Future perfect... Active voice... I will have beaten him.

Passive voice.... He will have been beaten by me.

Change of voice in the simple present.

Active voice... He reads a novel.

Passive voice.. A novel is read by him.

Active voice... He does not obey his teachers.

Passive voice.... His teachers are not obeyed by him.

Active voice.... Why do you waste time?

Passive voice..... Why is time wasted by you?

Active voice... Who teaches you physics?

Passive voice.... By whom are you taught physics?

Active voice... Which book do you read these days?

Passive voice... Which book is read by you these days?

Past Simple Tense

Active voice.... He did not help me.

Passive voice.. I was not helped by him.

Active voice... I told him a story.

Passive... A story was told to her by me.

Present Perfect Tense.

Active... Has he done his work?

Passive.. Has his work been done by him?

Active... She has read this book.

Passive... The book has been read by her.

Active... Who has stolen my watch?

Passive... By whom has my watch been stolen?

Active... Have you not solved this sum?

Passive... Has this sum not been solved by you?

Active... He has not helped me.

Passive.. I have not been helped by him.

Past Perfect Tense.

Active... She had already cooked the food.

Passive... The food had already been cooked by him.

Active... Had he not read this letter. ?

Passive... Had this letter not been read by him?

Active... Whose team had won the match?

Passive... By whose team had the match been won?

Active.... Hadn't he done his homework.

Passive… Hadn't his homework been done by him?

Future Perfect Tense.

Active... He will have received the letter before you reach there.

Passive... The letter will have been received by him before you reach there.

Active....She will not have washed the clothes by this time.

Passive... The clothes will not have been washed by her by this time.

Active... Will the gardener have watered plants before 5pm.

Passive... Will the plants have been watered by the gardener before 5pm.

Active... The peon will have locked the main gate by 10pm.

Passive....The main gate will have been locked by the main peon by 10pm.

Imperative Sentences.

Imperative sentences Express command, order, request, suggestion, etc. while changing imperative sentences into the passive voice, we use verbs like, request, order etc.

Active- please post this letter.

Passive-You are requested to post this letter.

Active-Shut the door.

Passive-You are ordered to shut the door.

Modal Auxiliaries.

The form of the passive sentences will be modal+be+pastparticiple.

Active... You can do this work.

Passive.. This work can be done by you.

Active... He may help you.

Passive... You may be helped by him.

Active....She might win the match.

Passive... The match might be won by her.

Active....Could you lend me fifty rupees?

Passive... Could fifty rupees be lent to me by you.

Active... He should respect his elders.

Passive..... His elders should be respected by him.

Quasi-Passive

Active... This mango tastes sweet.

Passive.. This mango is sweet when tasted.

Active.. The shop is building.

Passive.. The shop is being built.

Active... The rose smells sweet.

Passive.. The rose is sweet when smelt.

Active... Your shirt needs washing.

Passive.. Your shirt needs to be washed.

Active.. This medicine tastes bitter.

Passive.. This medicine is bitter when tasted

Miscellaneous Examples.

Active... Grass grows over the fields.

Passive....The fields are over grown with grass.

Active... Someone has stolen my pen.

Passive.. My pen has been stolen.

Active....People say that he is a rich man.

Passive....It is said that he is a rich man.

Active... It is time to ring the bell.

Passive... It is time for the bell to be rung.

Active...Your behaviour surprises me.

Passive.. I am surprised at your behaviour

Active... I know him.

Passive.. He is known to me.

Active....music interests me.

Passive... I am interested in music.

Active... This bottle contains milk.

Passive... milk is contained in this bottle.

Active... Twelve months make a year.

Passive.. A year is made of twelve months.

Active.. One must do one's duty.

Passive....Duty must be done.

Exercise

Change the following sentences into passive voice.

1. He has missed the train.

The train has been missed by him.

2. Do they speak French?

Is French spoken by them?

3. was he reading a book?

Was a book being read by him?

4. compose this letter.

Let this letter be composed.

5. where did you buy this pen from?

From where was this pen bought from?

6. who wrote this speech?

By whom was this speech written?

7. one should respect one's elders.

Elders should be respected.

8. I did not praise anybody.

Nobody was praised by me.

9. He hurt his leg in an accident.

His leg was hurt in an accident.

10. Someone was knocking at the door.

The door was being knocked at by someone.

Question no 1.

Change the voice of the following sentences from Active to passive.

1. Rohan is playing cricket.

2. Ramesh is singing a song.

3. Uma is writing a letter.

4. They are watching T.V.

5. The workers are making a wall.

6. The P. W. D is constructing this building.

7. She is eating a banana.

8. Are you reading this novel?

9. When are they sending the gift?

10. Who is chasing them?

(Answer)

1. Cricket is being played by Rohan.

2. A song is being sung by Ramesh.

3. A letter is being written by Uma.

4. T.V. is being watched by them.

5. A wall is being made by the workers.

6. This building is being constructed by P.W.D.

7. A banana is being eaten by her.

8. Is this novel being read by you?

9 when is the gift being sent by them?

10. Who are they being chased by?

Question No 2.

Passive to Active.

1. I am being disturbed by you.

2. He is not being teased by them.

3. Are you being trained by him.

4. sixes after sixes are being hit by Virat Kohli.

5. A lot of time is being wasted by them.

6. Wide balls are being bowled by Ishant Sharma.

7. Are they being chased by someone?

8. Holi is being celebrated by all.

9. A letter is being written to the president of India by them.

10. Who is being given the charge by them?

(Answer)

1. You are disturbing me.

2. They are not teasing him.

3. Is he training you?

4. Virat Kohli is hitting sixes after sixes.

5. They are wasting a last of time.

6. Ishant Sharma is bowling wide balls.

7. Is anybody chasing them?

8. All are celebrating Holi.

9. They are writing a letter to the president of India.

10. Who are they giving the charge to?

Question No 3.

Present Perfect Tense Active to Passive.

1. They have bought school uniform.

2. The doctors have operated upon him.

3. Ali has made peace with his friends.

4. Pratima has visited the doctor.

5. Measles has infected parul.

6. I have brought lots of sweets.

7. She has finished her work.

8. Mohan has invited shobha.

9. They have not prepared the project.

10. Have they completed the task?

(Answer)

1. School uniform has been bought by them.

2. He has been operated upon by the doctors.

3. Peace has been made by Ali with his friends.

4. The doctor has been visited by Partima.

5. Parul had been infected by measles.

6. Lots of sweets have been brought by me.

7. Her work has been finished by her.

8. Shobha has been invited by Mohan.

9. The project has not been prepared by them.

10. Has the task been completed by them?

Question No 4.

Passive to Active.

1. The violin has been played by me.

2. Home work has been done by me.

3. Lunch has been eaten by the children.

4 The car has been cleaned by them.

5. The shoes have been polished by me.

6. Justice has been done to victims.

7. This has been known to me for a long time.

8. A beautiful dress has been purchased by me.

9. Has a safari been experienced by you.

10. The movie has been seen by them on Monday.

(Answer)

1. I have played the violin.

2. I have done home work.

3. The children have eaten lunch.

4. They have cleaned the car.

5. I have polished the shoes.

6. Victims have been done justice.

7. I have known this for a long time.

8. I have purchased a beautiful dress.

9. Have you experienced a safari.

10. They have seen the movie on Monday.

Question No 5.

Active to Passive.

1. I ate my dinner alone.

2. Rina took the car.

3 I used the subway, to cross the road.

4. I saw them going towards the temple.

5 Rani cleaned the entire floor.

6. I planted these trees.

7. She drank the whole glass of milk.

8. He booked a seat for me last week.

9. Why did you not help him?

10. I needed a break from work.

(Answer)

1. Dinner was eaten by me alone.

2. The car was taken by Rina.

3. The subway was used by me to cross the road.

4. They were seen by me going towards the temple.

5. The entire floor was cleaned by Rani.

6. These trees were planted by me.

7. The whole glass of milk was drunk by her.

8. A seat was booked for me last week by him.

9. Why was he not helped by you?

10. A break from work was needed by me.

Question No 6.

1. The plants were watered by the gardener.

2. Dinner was eaten by me.

3. The song was sung by me.

4. The painting was made by him.

5. He was praised by his father.

6. Yoga was learnt by the students.

7. The secret was known to my mother.

8. The poem was written by Byron.

9. I was shouted at by the neighbours.

10. The facts were denied by the witnesses in the court.

(Answer)

1. Gardener watered the plants.

2. I ate dinner.

3. I sang the song.

4. He made the painting.

5. His father praised him.

6. The students learnt yoga

7. My mother knew the secret.

8. Byron wrote the poem.

9. The neighbours shouted at me.

10. The witnesses denied the facts in the court.

Question No 7.

Past Continuous Tense Active to Passive.

1. Vidit was taking all the prescribed medicines.

2. The tourists were visiting the beautiful city.

3. They were playing the match fairly.

4. I was watching the match.

5. Mother was cooking vegetables.

6 I was enjoying the day.

7. The birds were building a nest in the oak tree.

8. I was riding the horse.

9. Saina was playing golf.

10. I was learning swimming.

(Answer)

1. All the prescribed medicines were being taken by Vidit.

2. The beautiful city was being visited by tourists.

3. The match was being played fairly by them.

4. The match was being watched by me.

5. Vegetables were being cooked by the mother.

6. A nest was being built by the birds in the oak tree.

7. The day was being enjoyed by me.

8. The horse was being ridden by me.

9. Golf was being played by Saina.

10. Swimming was being learnt by me.

Question No 8.

Passive to Active.

1. This work had been done by Tina.

2. The attack had been planned by the terrorists.

3. The sheets had been changed by the maid.

4. The game had been played well by both the teams.

5. The tax had been paid by Lata.

7. The music had been stopped by uncle.

8. The bicycle had been ridden by me.

9. The ground had been damaged by the rain.

10. Dust had been cleaned by me.

11. The pizza had been ordered by me.

(Answer)

1. Tina had done this work.

2 The terrorists had planned the attack.

3. The maid had charged the sheets.

4. Both the teams had played the game well.

5. lata had paid the tax.

6. uncle had stopped the music.

7. I had ridden the bicycle.

8. The rain had damaged the ground.

9. I had cleaned the dust.

10. I had ordered the pizza.

NARRATION

1. Direct and indirect speech.

The words spoken by a person can be reported in two ways -Direct and indirect. When we quote the exact words spoken by a person, we call it direct speech.

Sohan said to Mohan, "I am going to school."

The exact words spoken by Sohan are put within inverted commas. But when we give the substance of what Sohan said, it is called the indirect speech.

2. Reporting clause and Reported speech.

Sohan told Mohan that he was going to school. The words which generally come before the inverted commas are called the reporting clause, Sohan said to Mohan and the verb 'said, 'is called the reporting verb.

The words spoken by Sohan and put within inverted commas are called the reported speech, "I am going to school."

3. Rules for changing direct speech into indirect speech

In the indirect speech, no inverted commas are used.

The conjunctions that, if, whether, are generally used after the reporting verb. The first word of the reported speech begins with a capital letter.

The tense of the reporting verb is never changed.

The reporting verb changes according to sense. It may be told, asked, inquired etc.

4. Rules for the change of pronouns.

The first person pronouns (I, me, my, we us, our)in the reported speech change according to the subject of the reporting verb.

The pronouns of the second person (you, your, yourself)in the reported speech change according to the subject of the reporting verb.

The pronouns of the third person do not change.

Expample.

1. He said, "I like the book"

He said that he liked the book.

2. He said to me "Do you like the book"

He asked me if I liked the book.

Change in tenses.

If the reporting verb is in the present or the future tense, the tense of the reported speech is not changed.

Satish says, "I am flying a kite."

Satish says that he is flying a kite.

Satish will say, "I want a glass of milk."

Satish will say that he wants a glass of milk.

If the reporting verb is in the past tense, then the tense of the reported speech will change as follows.

Simple present to simple past.

Present progressive......am/is/are writing

Present perfect

Has written

Simple past

Wrote

Past progressive

Was/were writing

Past progressive

Was/were writing

Past perfect

Had written

Past perfect progressive had been writing.

If the direct speech expresses a historical fact, a universal.

Changing statements into indirect speech.

The reporting verb "said to is changed to 'told', replied, remarked."

The reporting verb is not followed by an object, it is not changed.

The inverted commas are removed. The conjunction 'that' is used to connect the reporting clause with the reported speech. The rules of the change of pronouns, tenses, etc. are followed.

Ramu said, "I saw a lion in the forest."

Ramu said that he had seen a lion in the forest.

Satish said to me, "I am very happy here."

Satish told me that he was very happy there.

He said, "I can do this work."

He said that he could do that work.

Renu said to me, "I was washing the clothes."

Renu told me that she had been washing the clothes."

She said, "I am not well."

She said that she was not well.

He said to Sita, "I have passed the test."

He told Sita that he had passed the test.

I said to my friend, "He has been working very hard."

I told my friend that he had been working very hard.

My friend said to me, "I shall go to Delhi tomorrow."

My friend told me that he would go to Delhi the next day.

I said, "I agree to what he said."

I said that I agreed to what he had said.

The student said to the teacher, "I am sorry that I am late."

The student told the teacher that he was sorry that he was late.

Rules for the change of interrogative (questions)sentences.

The reporting verb 'say' is changed into ask, inquire.

The interrogative sentence is changed into a statement by placing the subject. before the verb and the full stop is put of the end of the sentence.

If the interrogative sentence has a wh-word (who, when, where, how, why, what etc.)the wh-word is repeated in the sentence. It serves as a conjunction. If the interrogative sentence is a yes no answer type sentence (with auxiliary verbs is am, are, was, were, do, did, have, shall, etc.), then if or whether is used as a conjunction.

The auxiliaries do, does, did, in a positive question in the reported speech are dropped.

The conjunction that is not used after the reporting clause.

Changing commands and requests into indirect speech.

In imperative sentences having commands, the reporting verb is changed into command, order, tell, allow, request etc.

The imperative mood is changed into the infinitive mood by putting to before the verb in case of negative sentences, the auxiliary 'do' is dropped and 'to' is placed after 'not'.

She said to me, "Open the window."

She ordered me to open the window.

The captain said to the soldiers, "Attack the enemy."

The captain commanded the soldiers to attack the enemy.

I said to him, "leave this place at once."

I told him to leave that place at once.

The teacher said to the students, "listen to me attentively."

The teacher asked the students to listen to him attentively.

Exercise

1. He said, "I will do it now."

2. He says, "Honesty is the best policy."

3. Ramesh says, "I have written a letter."

4. She said, "Mahesh will be reading a book."

5. She said, "Where is your father?"

6. He said to me, "please take your book."

7. The principal said to the peon, "let this be go out."

8. He said to me, "May you live long."

9. She said, "Good by friends."

10. The students said, "Alas! wasted my time last year."

CLAUSE

Clause... The basic sentence unit.

The sentence is considered to be the largest unit of grammar, but the clause is the core unit of grammar. A sentence is made up of one or more clauses. A clause has its own subject and predicate.

Sentences with one clause... subject... he

Predicate......came to my house.

Subject....I

Predicate....was reading then.

Sentences with more than one clause... subject.. I

Predicate 1+subject 2

Was reading. When he is the man.

Predicate 2

Came my house.

Saved me that day.

A clause is a group of words with a subject predicate structure forming a part of sentence or a complete sentence.

Clauses are three types.

1. Main/principal clause.

2. Subordinate/Dependent clause.

3. Coordinate Clause

It is grammatically dependent on another clause.

It complete the statement it sector develops some aspects of the statement.

When I finished the work, I took a little rest.

As he heard the news, he ran to hospital.

Sentence

(1)Main clause... I saw the thing.

(2)Subordinate clause.....when I came here.

Coordinate clause

A Coordinate clause is a clause that is linked to a clause of the by a coordinating conjunction.

Coordinate clause coordinating conjunction.

Sentence

I finished the work and took a little rest.

I finished....coordinate clause.

and..... coordinating conjunction.

3. Coordinate clause.

A clause that can form a sentence on its own is called a main clause.

Sentences have two clauses.

1. main clause... I saw the thing

A coordinate clause is a clause that is linked to a clause of the by a coordinating conjunction.

He could be very loving as the world turn very strict.

Types of subordinate clause... 1. noun clause 2. adjective clause 3. adverb clause.

The noun clause that functions like a noun in a main clause is called a noun or nominal clause.

Function of noun clause

Like a noun it works as the subject, object, complement or an appositive in a main clause.

Noun clause is linked to the main cause with nominal conjunction.

Function of the noun clause.

subject of a verb..... That he is an honest man is known to us.

What he said is true.

When he will come is uncertain. What you want is a cup of tea.

Adverb clause

The clause that functions like an adverb or adverbial is called an adverb clause.

An adverb clause is linked to a companion clause with a subordinate conjunction. After, as, it, when, since, though, before, because, unless, while, until, where although adverb clause.

Functions

Modifies a verb....He was punished because he behaved wrongly.

When he came, I was reading.

It rains, they will come late.

Ashewas ill, he couldn't go to school.

We eat so that we may live.

Unless you work hard you will fail.

Though he tried hard, he could not succeed.

Modifies an adjective

He is so poor that he cannot buy his books.

The story is so exciting that I can't describe.

I am so tired that I can't walk.

He is as dull as he is lazy.

She is younger than she looks.

Modifies an adverb..... He drinks as greedily as he eats.

He behaved so harshly that we were all ashamed.

He does the work more quickly than I can do.

He did it so promptly that we couldn't believe.

Exercise

Try to identify the main clause and subordinate clause from the following sentences.

1. This is what I wanted.

2. This is the thing that I wanted.

3. I know who has done it.

4. If you come, I shall go to your house.

5. It is true that he has not done it.

6. When he came here, I was sleeping.

7. He was punished as he was late.

8. This is the dog who told me the thing.

9. The dog that bites does not bark.

10. We eat so that we may live.

Find out the nominal clause is the following sentences and determine their function in the main clause.

1. He told me that you were not in the office.

2. That he is an honest man is known to all.

3. I know that he will help you.

4. We hope that he will be soon here.

5. This is what all know.

Point out the adjective clauses in the following sentences and determine their antecedents.

1. The man who sits by the principal is my father.

2. Tell me the time when they will come here.

3. This is the pen you gave me.

4. I know the man who stole your watch.

5. This is the place where Tagore was born.

6. The man who came here yesterday is his uncle.

7. The boy who helped me that day is here.

8. I have a mobile phone which made in Japan.

9. Tell me the place where we went.

10. The thing you gave me is lost.

Find out the adverbial clause is following sentences.

1. He was so kind that I can't Express in words.

2. We are working hard so that we can achieve our target.

3. He is much older than he looks.

JOINING SENTENCES

What is a sentence?

A sentence is a group of words that contains at least one subject and one predicate and makes complete sense.

Note: A sentence starts with a capital letter and ends with a full stop.

Example..A good business man maintains good relations with his customer. Sometimes the subject may be absent or implied.

Example..Thank you. (I thank you)

Sentence can be categorized into four types.

A sentence that is a statement or assertion and ends with a period is called Declarative sentence.

A sentence that gives directions or command and ends with a period is called Imperative sentence.

A sentence that asks question and ends with a question mark is called interrogative sentence.

A sentence that shows strong emotion and ends with an exclamation mark is called exclamatory sentence.

Synthesis of Sentences.

Synthesis of sentences means combination of a number of simple sentences into one new sentence. That new sentence might be either simple sentence or a compound sentence or a complex sentence.

Simple Sentence.

A simple sentence contains a subject and a predicate. It expresses a complete thoughts.

Example.. The boys went to the park.

Compound Sentence.

A compound sentence contains two or more independent clause. These clauses are joined by a coordinating conjunction.

Example... The boys went to the park, but they did not go to the zoo.

Complex Sentence.

A complex sentence contains one or more dependent clauses and least one independent clause. In addition to the subject and a verb a subordinating conjunction or a similar word in also present.

Example of subordinating conjunction are although, whereas, whoever else.

Combining two or more simple sentences into one simple sentence.

1. By using a participle

Example.. He jumped up. He ran away.

Jumping up, he ran away.

He was tired to play. He sat down to rest.

2. By using a noun or phrase in apposition.

Example.. This is my friend. His name is Rama.

This is my friend Rama.

I spent two days in London. It is one of the most attractive place in England.

Buddhism was founded 2500 years ago. It is one of the greatest religious. Buddhism one of the greatest religious was founded 2500 years ago.

3. By using a preposition with noun or gerund.

Example.. The moon rose. Their journey was not ended.

The moon rose before their journey ended.

He has failed many times. he still hopes to win.

Having failed for many times, he still hopes to win.

By using, nominative absolute construction.

Example.. The soldiers arrived. The mob dispersed. The soldiers having arrived, the mob dispersed.

The town was enclosed by strong wall.

The enemy was unable to capture it.

The town having been enclosed by strong wall, the enemy was unable to capture it.

By using an Infinitive.

Example... I have some duties. I must perform them.

We must finish this exercise. There are still three sentences.

We still have three sentences in this exercise to finish.

By using an adverb or an Adverbial Phrase.

Example... He deserved to succeed. He failed. He failed undeservedly.

The sunset. The boys had not finished the game.

The boys had not finished the game by sunset.

3. Alternative conjunctions (or, either, nor, neither.. nor, otherwise, else etc.)

These conjunctions are used when two alternative facts or statements have to be presented.

Example... you can have tea.

You can have coffee.

You can have tea (or) coffee.

He doesn't smoke. He does not drink.

He (neither) smokes (nor) drinks.

You must apologize. You will be punished.

You must apologize, (otherwise) you will be punished.

4. Relative conjunctions (therefore, for, so etc.) These are used when an inference from another statement or fact has to be made.

Example... He must be asleep. The lights are off.

He must be asleep (for)the lights are off.

He has been working hard. he will pass.

He has been working hard (therefore) he will pass.

Combination of two or more simple sentences to form a single complex sentence.

1. Subordinate clause as a noun clause. in the following examples, the subordinate clause is a noun clause.

Example.. you are drunk. That aggravates your offense.

That you are drunk aggravates your offense.

He will be late. That is certain.

It is certain that he will be late.

You are repentant. I will not forget it.

I will not forget that you are repentant

He may be innocent. I do not know.

I do not know whether he is innocent.

2. Subordinate clause as an Adjective clause.

In the following examples, the subordinate clause is an Adjective clause.

Example... I met an old man. He was very weak.

I met an old man who was very weak.

She keeps her ornaments in a safe. That is safety locker.

I saw a car. It was blue in colour.

I saw a car which was blue in colour.

3. Subordinate clause as an Adverb clause.

Example... Indira Gandhi died in 1984. Rajiv Gandhi, thereafter became the prime minister of India. When Indira Gandhi died in 1984, Rajiv Gandhi became the prime minister of India.

I waited for my friend. I waited till his arrival.

I waited for my friend until he arrived.

He fled somewhere. His pursuers couldn't follow him.

He fled where his pursuers couldn't follow him.

Tell me the truth I shall pardon you.

I shall pardon you if you tell me the truth.

1. Combine each of the following pairs of sentences into a simple sentence.

He won a jackpot. He built a big mansion.

He stood on tip-toe. He reached for the bunch of grapes.

He is going to London. He wants to pursue higher education there.

Milton was the homer of England. He wrote paradise lost.

Patel was a strong man. He brought all the princely states into the Indian union. He used the method of persuasion. Sometimes he used the method of coercion.

Gandhi was a great visionary. He realized the danger of communal conflicts. He sacrificed his life to bring about unity.

2. Combine each of the following pairs of sentences into compound sentences.

The cow boy had made millions of dollars.

He had also lost the du.

One day he walked into my office. he had a contract in his hand.

The spate was bigger. She could see it from for.

India sheltered Dalai lama. His life would have been in danger.

Exercise was not something you took. It was something you got.

3. Combine each of the following Paris of sentences into complex sentences.

Exercise

School was over. It was a celebration.

She read anne's diary. She was moved to write a Otto.

Transformation of sentences with answers.

He is too weak to walk.

He is so weak that he cannot walk.

The news is too good to be true.

The news is so good that it can't be true.

He is too clever to be easily deceived.

He is so clever that he cannot be easily deceived.

No sooner had I reached the station than the train arrived.

As soon as I reached the station the train arrived.

Hardly had I reached the station when the train arrived.

No sooner had the meeting begun that the protesters rushed to the platform.

As soon as the meeting began the protesters rushed to the platform.

Hardly had the meeting begun when the protesters rushed to the platform. Scarcely had the meeting begun when the protesters rushed to the platform.

Interchange of the degrees of comparison positive, comparative.

I am as strong as him. (positive degree)

He is not stronger than me. (Comparative degree)

This razor is not as sharp as that one. (positive degree)

That razor is sharper than this one. (comparative degree).

Very few cities in India are as rich as Mumbai. (Positive)

Mumbai is richer than most of the other cities in India. (Comparative)

Mumbai is one of the richest cities in India (superlative)

Interchange of one part of speech with another.

He succeeded in his attempt. (Succeeded verb)

His attempt was met with success. (success noun)

Conversion of a simple sentence into a compound sentence.

A simple sentence can be converted into a compound sentence by enlarging a word or a phrase into a coordinate clause.

Simple-climbing up the tree, he plucked some mangoes.

Compound....He climbed up the tree and plucked some mangoes.

Simple-Being ill, he didn't attend the party.

Compound-He was ill and didn't attend the party.

Simple... Besides being party, she is cleaner.

Compound-She is not pretty but also clever.

Compound-She is not only pretty but also clever.

Transformation of compound sentence into a simple sentence.

We can convert a compound sentence into a simple sentence by reducing the number of clauses into one.

Compound -He got up and walked away.

Simple... Getting up, he walked away.

Compound-He gave them not only a house but some land also.

Simple-Besides a house, he gave them some land also.

Compound -He ran away and thus escaped arrest.

Simple-He ran away in order to escape arrest.

Transformation of a simple sentence into a complex sentence.

Simple sentence can be converted into a complex sentence by expanding a word or phrase into a subordinate clause, which can be a noun clause, an adjective clause or an adverbial clause.

Noun Clause

Simple-He liked my suggestion.

Complex-He liked what I suggested.

Simple-There I saw a beautiful girl.

Complex-There I saw a girl who was beautiful.

Adverb Clauses.

Simple-She was too poor to educate her children.

Complex-She was so poor that she couldn't educate her children.

Conversion of a complex sentence into a simple sentence.

A complex sentence can be converted into a simple sentence by reading a subordinate clause into a word or a phrase.

Adjective Clause.

Complex... Those that are helpless deserve our pity.

Simple....The helpless deserve our pity.

Adverb Clause

Complex... They took shelter under a tree because they were driven by the rain.

Simple... Driven by the rain, they took shelter under a tree.

Conversion of compound to complex.

A compound sentence can be converted into a complex sentence, by changing an independent clause into a dependent clause.

Compound... search his pockets and you will find the watch.

Complex... If you search his pockets, you will find the watch.

Compound... Do as I tell you, or you will regret it.

Complex... Unless you do as I tell you, you will regret it.

Compound... The lion was wounded but not killed.

Complex... Although the lion was wounded, it was not killed.

The Gerund.

Read this sentence:

Reading is his favourite past time.

The word reading is formed from the verb read, by adding... ing.

We also see that it is here used as the subject of a verb, and hence does the work of a noun. It is, therefore, a verb-Noun, and is called a Gerund.

Further examples of Gerund:

1. Hunting tigers is a favourite sport in this country.

2. I like reading poetry.

He is fond of Harding money.

In sentence 1, the gerund, like a noun, is the subject of a verb but, like a verb, it also takes an object, thus clearly showing that it has also the force of a verb.

In sentence 2, the Gerund, like a noun is the object of a verb but, like a verb, it also takes an object, thus clearly showing that it has also the force of a verb.

In sentence 3, the Gerund like a noun, is governed by a preposition, but, like a, verb, it also takes an object.

It will be noticed that the infinitive and the Gerund are alike in being used as nouns while still retaining the power that a verb has of governing another noun or pronoun in the objective case.

Def--A Gerund is that form of the verb which ends in ing, and has the force of a Noun and a verb.

As both the Gerund and the Infinitive have the force of a Noun and a verb they have the same uses. Thus in many sentences either of them may be used without any special difference in meaning; as.

Teach me to swim.

Teach me swimming.

To give is better than to receive.

Giving is better than receiving.

The following sentences…

The present participle has force of an adjective and verb, it is a verbal adjective.

Examples of gerund....

He is fond of playing cricket.

The old man was tired of walking.

We were prevented from seeing the prisoner.

Seeing is believing.

Examples of participle......

Playing cricket, he gained health.

Walking along the road, he noticed a dead cobra.

Seeing, he believed.

Read this sentence.

The indiscriminate reading of novels is injurious.

The reading is used like an ordinary noun.

Notice that the is used before and of after it.

Further examples of gerunds used like ordinary nouns.

The making of the plants in hand.

The time of the singing of the birds has come.

Adam consented to the eating of the fruit.

The middle station of life seems to be the most advantageously situated for the gaining of wisdom.

In such compound nouns as

Walking stick, frying pan, Fencing stick, writing table, hunting whip, Walking, frying, hunting, fencing, writing are gerunds.

They mean "a stick for walking", "a pan for frying", "a whip for hunting" "a stick for fencing" and "a table for writing."

Of the following two sentences the first one is correct

1. I hope you will excuse my leaving early. (Correct)

2. I hope you will excuse me leaving early. (Incorrect)

The word leaving is a gerund (i.e. a noun), therefore it must be preceded by the possessive form.

Remember, therefore, to use the possessive case of nouns and pronouns before gerunds, as, Were juiced at his (not him)being promoted.

We heard of their (not them)having discovered another stream.

I have no faith in keeping his promise.

I insist on your being present.

We left without any one's knowing.

All depends on Karim's passing the examination.

The accident was due to the engine driver's disregarding the signals.

Exercise

1. He was found fighting desperately for his life.

2. He has ruined his sight by reading small print.

3. Hearing the noise, he ran to the window.

4. We saw a clown standing on his head.

5. Asking questions is easier than answering them.

6. Waving their hats and handkerchiefs, the people cheered the king.

7. Walking on the grass is forbidden.

8. Jumping over the fence, the thief escaped.

9. The miser spends his time in hoarding money.

10. Much depends on Rama's returning before noon.

11. Amassing wealth of ruins health.

12. I was surprised often Hari's being absent.

13. We spent the afternoon in playing cards.

14. The miser hated spending money.

15. Captain Hardy congratulated him on his having gained a complete victory.

PARAGRAPH

The season I like most.

All seasons come once in a cycle of one year. There are three important seasons in our country - summer, winter, and the rainy season. December and January are the coolest month and May and June are the hottest month of year. July and August brings heavily rains. Each season has its pleasure and pain. In India, the months of February and March. Are very pleasures and bring happiness with many festivals. This season is called 'spring'. The season spring I like the most. It is neither hot nor cold. It is the season of greenery, flowers, fruits, and festivals. The wind blows in its special way like playing with trees and having green leaves plants. It sings when passes through branches and leaves of trees and plants. In this season I feel healthy and fit.

The Rainy Season.

I like the rainy season most. It is also known as monsoon season. It is my favourite and best season among all four seasons. Rainy season starts in India in the month of June when winds of south west monsoon starts blowing. Monsoon begins in the middle of June and continues up to September. According to Hindu calendar this season is felt in the months of Ashadha and Shravana. During the season the sky is generally over cast with clouds. The clouds of different shades move in the sky and look very nice. Sometimes rain comes along with lightning and thunder. The Rainy season comes after the summer season. So, this season brings relief to the burning earth scorched in the summer heat. The temperature remains pleasant during this season.

All the trees and plants get covered with new green leaves and lawns and fields gets covered with the great looking green velvet grass. The beautiful rainbow falls in the sky. The sun plays hide and seek with the clouds. Peacocks and other forest birds start dancing in full swing by spreading their wings. In this season the rivers, canals, tanks and other low land are full of water. Rainy season is of great importance for the

Indian farmers as they really need more water for their crops cultivation. A large number of farmers depend upon monsoon rains to meet the food requirement of their family. They engage to fulfil the needs of their family. They engage in agricultural activities not to sell the crops but for their own needs too.

How I spend my Holiday

I spent my holiday to go on tour on a hill station with my parents for Shimla. It was very joy full and interesting tour for me. After packing our travel bag, We catch the bus from bus stand. After a journey of 8 hours we reached the Shimla and we booked a hotel to stay for three days. We saw many places and beauty of mountains. Really it is good and pleasant to see hills and its areas. After three days we came back to Delhi. I never forget this journey in my life.

A scene in the Bazaar.

The market of may town is very important. There is no other place of grain market in the area of so much brisk business as this market is. The market itself is in the centre of the town. All-important bazaars of the town.

I always find a big crowd there. Businessmen come from far and wide. They transact businesses. The market is always crowded with carts, horses, donkeys and camels. They come loaded with the produce of the season such as cotton, grain, oilseeds, gour and vegetables. These things are arranged in an attractive manner for sale. The merchants make their purchases moving in groups. They bid in a particular fashion. They do some indications under the clothes to fix the rates of the commodities brought in the day. In the evening all commodities are packed in the jute bags. They sent back to places where they are in demand. The country carts, horses and donkeys go back with their masters to the villages.

Value of Trees.

Plants and trees are an inseparable part of our lives and there would be no life on earth without then. Air on our planet would not be breathable but for trees and plants because they take in carbon dioxide from the air and let out oxygen. Besides this, the fertile upper layers of soil are held in place against blowing wind and the flowing water, by tree and plant roots. This prevent land from becoming infertile and turning into an arid desert. Forests of all types and varieties cover over 35 million Sq. km of our planet. Small seeds grow into plants and then gradually into bigger trees. Trees perform all the functions like a plant but on a much larger scale. Growth takes place mainly at the ends of tree.

Trunks grow from within and a cross section of trees trunks would show rings of light and dark coloured wood. One dark and one light coloured ring signifies a year of growth, that is why the age of a tree can be calculated by counting the number of rings in side its trunk. As the trunk grows it forms a rough scaly surface on the outside called a 'bark'. Young trees have smoother barks, but as trees grow older the bark becomes scaly, cracks and eventually falls off. New bark is in the mean while being generated from within a tree's bark prevents the inner wood from losing water and drying out and protects the tree from fungus and moulds. Since food from trees can be put to a very large number of used, constant cutting down of trees should be awarded.

Life in a big city.

The city life of a big city is always growing and moving. Also, there are hundreds and thousands of opportunities for people in big cities to learn and grow. In addition, they provide a chance to grow professionally and personally. Due to the exposure in cities, people tend to be smarter and intelligent in comparison to the people who live in small towns and villages. Besides, the life of the city is very fast and only people with smart minds can survive there. The scope of personal growth and development is more in comparison to towns and villages. Furthermore, the children of big cities have access to better school and colleges which give them an opportunity for all round development.

A visit to the Hill Station.

During my last summer vacation, I paid a visit to Shimla where my elder brother lives. He is a forest officer there. I planned to go there in summer as the plains at that time are very hot. I boarded the Kalka mail at Amritsar on the 15th of June. Our train reached Kalka at 5:30 next morning. Then I changed for Shimla. Our journey to Shimla was through hilly area. The train took a zigzag track. The air was cool, fresh and pleasant. I felt that it was quite different from the scorching heat of Amritsar. The scenery on the either side of railway track was very charming. The train passed through several tunnels. I reached Shimla at about 2 pm. My elder brother and my sister in law were at the Shimla station.

I went out for long walk every morning and evening. I inhaled the healthful mountain air. going up and coming downhill gave me a good exercise. This exercise increased my hunger. I did full justice to my food during my stay at Shimla.

A visit to Historical Monument.

Our school arranged a trip to Agra last week on Saturday. We started this tour by bus via Taj Express. It was three days trip. We were very eager to see the beauty of the Taj Mahal. It is situated at the bank of Yamuna River. After enjoying a very comfortable journey of about two hours, we reached Agra. We stayed here is a big hotel, which was in Agra city. Here, first we took lunch and went for Taj Mahal. All of us were surprised to see the real beauty of the Taj Mahal as we had already read and heard about its wonder. It was really the wonder of world. Using of white marble was great to see for me as a visitor. Our guide explained to us each part of this historical monument in details with the story of Shahjahan and his wife Mumtaz Mahal. It was really a sweet memorial. Our next visit was for the Red fort of Agra and Fatehpur Sikri. We were very happy to see these all historical places and this trip was very successful as it was educative and entertaining.

Work is Worship.

Working is natural character of human beings. He lives a great life by doing work and makes his life meaning full. His life goes through many difficulties and happiness and thus he gets success. So it is said that work is the key to success. All great persons have made keep to work and presented many ideals to the people to get success as they achieved. Man is the crown of creation only because he has skill capable to find the way in any difficulties by hard work. using logical conclusion a man can decide what is beneficial for him. Thus his mind guides him to do right work. Humans have developed very fast than other creature make weapons to their work. It was not possible without hard work even we can't think.

Advantage and disadvantage of Science.

Science is the system of systematic knowledge based on facts and human experiences. The science of the Latin word "Scientia" meaning, the "knowledge".

The advantages of science and technology are:

1. It will make our life easier.

2. It helps us organize our daily activities.

3. This helps our work to be done faster.

4. It helps us to communicate more easily with others.

5. This helps us to better know and understand other cultures and societies. By discovering science, scientists are able to create something that can immeasurably improve the quality of life, for example computers, telephones, televisions planes and the list go on. with the discovery of these inventions, people can achieve their aspiration.

The disadvantages of Science And Technology.

1. It can be easily handled by irresponsible people.

2. We will be too dependent on that. When technology fails, we are helpless.

3. Sometimes it affects our health and our life styles (we will be complacent and lazy. Chemicals are dangerous)

4. It destroys our simple and healthy life (the traditional life style I miss)

5. Invasion of our private life.

If on the one hand, science and technology have brought us a lot of wonders, on the other hand, there are also disadvantages of science and technology. First, it has increased anxiety in our lives. second, when technology falls into the wrong hands, it can have a negative impact on society, such as the rising rate of cyber criminality, hacking, theft of formulae.

Save Tiger

Tigers are endemic species now a day in the world. There are very few numbers of tigers remain to see. This is very sensitive matter. But these are not enough. There are many national parks and sanctuary in India to protect them. Conservation of wild life is very important for all human beings as it will produce imbalance in environment. Tigers have now become a topic of interest and issue all over the world. The numbers of tigers decreasing day by day not only in India but also in the world. Tigers are our national animal. Recently, there are only 1411 tigers left in India.

It is said in a report. They always face the cruelty by some people for different purposes like skin for medicine, hunter for pleasure and deforestation is the main cause of this. India government has made plan for conservation the wild life but this is not enough. There are no so much lands for animals to survive, so that most of animals are in danger.

A major parts of jungle's land is being occupied for industrialisation, agriculture as well as mining. This is fact that tigers are not only in danger but also nature is in danger. Forest is natural habitats of wild life. So we have to save tigers swells forests. we always see around us cruelty and inhumanity by some people for animals. So we need love for them and some work to protect them.

A visit to a Zoo.

Last Sunday, the weather was pleasant. I along with my family, visited zoo. It is situated at a distance of twenty kilometres from our house. When we reached the gate of the zoo, there was huge crowd there. People were buying entrance tickets. Some of them were sharing their excitement about the visit of the zoo. We reached there at 11:30am. We bought our tickets and went inside the zoo. There were a large number of people there. we first visited zoological garden. There we saw a huge lake in which different types of water birds were swimming. The sight of white duck swimming on the smooth surface of clean water was a wonderful delight. Then we moved ahead to the enclosure. Where playing birds were chirping.

Then we came across a big garden in which stags and deer's were frisking about. These animals were very active, sharp and smart. In one corner of the garden there was a big tree on which a large number of monkeys and baboons were jumping. Their tricks and pranks were very pleasing. Some people threw bananas at them to which they immediately tried to catch by jumping down the branches. children were enjoying by making faces at them. We next halted at an aquarium. There were varieties of aquatic animals and birds there. There were many species of fish. Their fidgeting in water was really very delighting. Next to this enclosure were kept polar bears who looked deserted and dejected. Then we moved to a big tank which was full of crocodiles.

Books are our good friends.

Books are not only student's good friends but they are also good friends of book lovers. These are the best sources of knowledge as well as important element of education. Our other friends cannot come to help us anytime but the books are those friends which come anytime to educate us whenever we call. As our life is joyless without friends similarly we are useless without book. We cannot ask any problem to friends and teachers but books reply us. They also make our life easy.

There are many types and size of books in the world like educational books, literature book, novels, The story books, The poem books, The epics, comics and so many other books those have knowledge. There are many books which are written in different languages. The history of books is very ancient. Books store knowledge related to universe and experiences of people. Now the knowledge and experience on internet is known as eBook. Books always stand by us to help us. A person never feels alone in the company of books as books have interesting contents, wonders and entertainment materials. It is often seen a person in journey feels loneliness then he buys books for reading. This proves books are our good friends.

The role of Social Media.

Now a days, social media has been very popular among everyone. It is the best medium to reach or share our feelings, problems, issues, thoughts, news, events as well as photos and videos to friends and followers. Social media is not only confined to you and me but also to politicians as well. Through different activities of politics our politicians are going to connect their people. This had brought social media into limelight in India. From previous two elections the role of social media has been very important as the party which has reached more activities and issues on these social media sites has won the elections. Regarding to this it can be said that social media has made conscious people as well as in creased their knowledge.

Junk Foods.

Junk foods mean the foods which are not good for health as well as body. They have great taste to eat and they look very appealing. It attracts to all age of people. It has very little nutritive content but extremely high calorie of sugar or trans-fat contents. Snacks fried food, chips, burger, pizza, samosa, soft drink and chowmin etc. examples of junk food. People especially young children get addicted to this junk food because of its appealing look and taste. It causes many chronic diseases like obesity, diabetes, heart problems as well as abdominal distress in which colic pain is common symptom. Junk food contains high quantity of animals fats which are unhealthy for our body. So we must have ourselves keep away from such food items to keep us healthy. We should provide our children homemade food.

Save Trees.

The Earth which we called mother has given us many gifts in which one of them is trees. Trees release oxygen which need for our life. Forest brings clouds and cause rainfall. Trees prevent soil erosion. They protect us from severe weather. They play very important role in maintaining balance in ecosystem. Trees not only give us flowers, fruits, timbers, fuels and herbal medicines but also provide us shade as well as relief from hot weather and give us fresh air. They only know to give not to take. Many of wild lives live in forests and they get their all need from trees. We also get our food from green plants. So trees are beautiful and useful gift of nature. There is rising a question. Should we cut down these tress to get our unnecessary requires? No, like trees offer us many things without any selfish reasons we should also protect them in same way. So "Save trees and save life."

Strengthening the CWSN

CWSN is the short name of children with special needs. Those children who are physically and mentally disabled need special care. There is the main role of their parents in the life of such children. They expect to us for love, care, sympathy with good education. In older time such children are killed or left carelessly to die. But now a days, the most people because of the proliferation of education have become aware. Parents feel change in their thoughts. They are aware for children medical care as well as education. In class room they face problem of learning as they may not be able to focus on the teacher during class room interaction. And their place of learning may vary. To overcome these problems of such children.

A friend in need a friend in deed.

A friend is person with whom one shares a bond of mutual respect affection and trust. Although typically two friends are not biologically related to each other, with time, they become a family. One of the most well-known phrases about friend ship goes like this "A Friend in need is a friend in deed." This phrase summarises the essence of true friendship. It means that friends who help each other at the time of need are real friends. Not everyone is lucky to have a true friend in life. A true friend is like a blessing. Such friend ship should always be treasured and nurtured with care.

The importance of a true friend......The importance of true friends in our life cannot be expressed in words.

A true friend ship is very giving and is equally joyous. spending time with our friends gives us a reason to laugh and celebrate life. A true friend ship inspires us to grow. Studies show that a healthy friendship improves and boosts self-confidence. A true friend tries his best to help a friend in his time of need. This may include one's emotional, physical or another needs. A friend helps you overcome your burden or difficulty by improving your morale, helping you however possible and providing advice. A true friend never quits our side for his own selfish needs and selflessly helps us without expecting any return. They act as our teacher, guide our confident and our companion. This doesn't mean that our friends don't criticize us.

When we find people with whom we can effectively communicate our thoughts and feelings we soon develop a bond that translates into friend ship and deep understanding. A friend ship cannot thrive without understanding. Thus, the saying "A friend in need is a friend in deed "describes what real friend ship is all about. In difficult times, we come to know the difference between true friends and pretentious friends. A friend ship which survives hard ships come out stronger. Friends who help us during hard times are truly assets to be hold.

Importance of Games and Sports.

Sports and games are very important for us. They keep us healthy and fit. They offer us a change from the monotony of daily life. It is useful means of entertainment and physical activity. Sports and games help in character building. They give us energy and strength. Sports and games are a means of mental and physical growth. They make us learn how to tackle the difficult situation. Sports develop sense of friendliness They develop in us the team spirit. They shape our body and make it strong and active. They give us energy and strength. They improve blood circulation. This improves our physical wellbeing. A sport is an integral part of education. Education without sports is in complete. These days sports are part of education.

Importance of Yoga in Modern Age.

Yoga is a gift of an ancient India. This is not only an ancient form of exercise but also it is a part of ancient India life style which evolved thousands of years back in the Indian society and is being practiced continuously since then. It is related to mental and physical fitness of body as well as it prevents from various forms of diseases and inabilities.

Actually it is develops for meditation which helps in relaxation of mind and body. Nowadays, yoga is not only being popular worldwide but also it has been joining to our daily life activity. Since last 15 years yoga has recovered the people from many mental and physical disability over the world and also replaced the medicines from the daily life. Yoga is considered as a carrier in young's, and are so many possibility for job in the world, Several universities added Yoga as a subject. Approximately 2 billion people around the world practice Yoga. Yoga is an ancient physical mental and spiritual practice that originated in India and is now practiced in various forms around the world. Indians have known the importance of yoga. People have known the importance and power of yoga over the period of time. There is another reason to adopt the yoga by various persons and countries. This is the busy life, stress full life and food mess problems. There are various forms of yoga that can be done by a person during his job works. A house wife also can do yoga in her kitchen. an office man also can practice in his office during work.

Rising Pollution.

Being aware of pollution is quite mandatory for all the students these days. In order to become a responsible citizen of the future world, every child should know how human activities are leaving an impact on the environment and nature. This topic is quite crucial. And school children should learn how to write an interesting essay on 'pollution' effortlessly. Take a glance below.

A few things to keep in mind...

1. Never ever hurry to write the essay.

2. Think properly and jot down your thoughts before proceeding.

3. Divide your write up into a few segments such as introduction, main body. (You can make a few points as per the topic)and conclusion.

4. Try writing short paragraphs.

Short and crisp sentences are…

Introduction

Pollution has become a very common yet serious issue in today's world. It has been there for a long time even before human evolution such as volcanic eruption, wild fire which lead to various. Photo chemical reactions in the atmosphere. The current concern is that it is rising day by day due to various resources of pollutants is human and human created machines. It is to say that pollution is damaging the mother earth severely and we humans, should play our part to prevent it from happening.

What is pollution?

Pollution they is the presence of contaminants in the natural environment that causes harm and damage and it lead to adverse changes.

Kinds of pollution.

There are mainly three kinds of pollution 1. Air pollution 2. Water 3.Land.

Independence Day.

India celebrates its Independence Day on 15th August every year. Independence Day reminds us of all the sacrifices that were made by our freedom fighters to make India free from British rule. On15th August 1947 India was declared. Independent from British colonialism and became the largest democracy in the world. In this essay on independence day, students will find all the important details of Indiana's independence history. They can refer to it for their exam preparation as essays are mostly asked in the CBSE English paper. Also they can use this essay as a speech for the independence day function at school. 15th August is celebrated as national festival with flag hoisting, parades and cultural events.

Schools, colleges, offices, society complexes, government and private organizations conduct functions and celebrate this day with great enthusiasm. On this day, the prime minister of India hoists the flag at the Red fort and addresses the nation by a speech. Doordarshan broadcasts the entire event live on television. Prime minister Pandit Jawharlal Nehru performed the first flag hoisting ceremony on 25th August 1947.

History of Independence day.

Britishers have ruled in India for almost 200 years. Under British rule, the lives of the people were miserable. India were treated as slaves and had no rights to say anything to them. Indian rules were mere puppets in the hands of British officers. Indian soldiers were treated inhumanely in British camps, and farmers were dying of starvation as they couldn't grow crops and had to pay land taxes.

Our freedom fighters struggled for India's independence. Famous leaders like Mahatma Gandhi, Subhash Chandra Bose, Bhagat Singh, Sardar Vallabhbhai Patel, Jawaharlal Nehru, Rani Laxmi Bai, Mangal Pandey, Dada Bhai Nauroji fought fearlessly against the Britishers. Many of them also sacrificed their lives to make India free from British rule. Their contribution and effort are remembered in India's independence history.

Why do we celebrate Independence day?

India achieved independence after years of struggle. India got complete freedom from the British and secured full autonomy on 15th August 1947. That's why the day holds great significance in the heart of every Indian citizen living in India or abroad. India has completed 73 years of freedom.

The use of Mobile Phones.

Mobile phone is one of the wonderful wonders of sciences. It has added a new dimension to our life and to communication system. It is a telephone system that works without any wire. It can be moved easily and quickly from place to place. Through mobile phone, we can send messages to distant places, play games and sports, know about time, solve the work of calculations, and are aware of different kinds of news and views. At present the popularity of the mobile phone is increasing. Many companies are also being setup for selling mobile phone. The price of mobile phone is also decreasing in comparison with the past. People are being encouraged to buy a mobile phone set at a cheaper rate.

Age of Advertisements.

There was a time when hawkers and vendors praised there good shouting as loudly as they could going from street to street, to draw the buyer's attention. The advertisements first appeared in the newspapers in forming the reader of the availability of particular stuff at particular store. Then came radio and cinema followed by many other modes of media. With the variety in media there was bound to be a variety in types of advertising. Different methods of advertising like pamphlets, hand bills, billboards, hoardings, slides and influencing sets of audio-video advertisements soon came up. Advertisements can now be made depending on the budget. The tough competition in the market has necessitated the need of advertising.

It is strange but true advertisements are popular with every age-group. Will it not be unjust to accept that advertisement do not influence our thinking and judgment when we rank ourselves as customers? More over the viewers today enjoy watching and entertainment programmes, through the style of advertisements have changed they have always held our attention.

The position of Women in India.

The position of women in ancient India has been a very complicated one because of the paradoxical statements, indifferent religious scriptures and sometimes in the same text at different places. Some have described their status ad 'equals to men', while others have held not only in disrespect but even in positive hatred. This is why it has presented many problems to sociologists while evaluating women's status in India. The cultural history of India reveals that India theoretically women enjoyed the status of Devi (goddess) as described in many religious texts of Hindus, the majority community in India.

Post-Vedic Period (Upanishads, Puranic and Smriti Periods).

The position enjoyed by women in Vedic period deteriorated in Pistvedic period. It was gradually degraded in the Puranic and Smriti periods. The description of position before BCE 300 shows that she enjoyed a fairly high status, though not to the extent that she enjoyed in Vedic period.

Amphan

The first tropical cyclone of the 2020 north Indian Ocean cyclone season, Amphan. originated from a low pressure area persisting a couple hundred miles (300km)east of Colombo, Sri Lanka, on 13 may 2020. Tracking northeast ward, the disturbance organized over exceptionally warm sea surface temperatures. The joint Typhoon warning centre (JTWC)upgraded the system to a tropical depression on 15th May while the India meteorological Department (IMD)followed suit the following day. on 17th May Amphan underwent rapid intensification and became an extremely severe cyclonic storm within 12 hours.

On 18th may, at approximately 12:00utc, Amphan reached its speak intensity with 3 minute sustained wind speeds of 240km/h(150mph), 1 minute sustained wind speeds of 260km/h(160mph) and a minimum central barometric pressure of 92 ombar (27. 17in Hg). The storm began an eye wall replacement cycle shortly after it reached its peak intensity, but the continued effects of dry air and wind shear disrupted this process and caused Amphan to gradually weaken as it paralleled the eastern coast line of India. On 20 may, between 10. 00 and 11. 00 UTC, the cyclone made land fall in west Bengal.

At the time, the JTWC estimated Amphan's 1 minute sustained winds to be 155km/h (95mph). Amphan rapidly weakened once inland and dissipated shortly thereafter coastal area in west Bengal comprising East midnapire, North 24 paraganas, south 24 paraganas, Kolkata, Hooghly, and Howraha as well as Odisha were affected by the cyclone. It also caused significant destruction in Bangladesh.

Politics in India.

Politics in any country involves the ruling party and the opposition. Usually and ideally, political parties are formed based on the same time of thinking and ideology. The left and the right are the two terms usually used by media and political commentators to define the group of people with the same ideological bend of mind. The lefts are usually considered majoritarian, pro poor and rebellious in nature.

These definitions are not defined anywhere in the constitutions, of any governmental organisations, but are the terms coined by journalists, authors and commentators. For example, in the USA, the Democrats are known to be left learning while the Republicans are known to be right learning, in UK labour party is seen to be right learning ideology and the conservative party having a left learning ideology. The case is similar in India as well, with Congress having left. learning ideologies while BJP having right learning ideologies. And for a perfect democracy to work, both the ideologies are necessary. A mature democracy is one where there is a fine demarcation between the two ideologies, but in countries like India these demarcations are not five in nature.

Child Labour.

Labour done by children for their living is child labour. Child labour represents a national shame and it is one of the biggest failures of the country. It is a great challenge that the country is facing today. The number of children engaged in child labour in India is higher than in any other developing countries. Poverty and illiteracy force families to send their children to work. The employers find its source of cheap and trouble free labour. Because children can be beaten and bullied. They can easily be thrown out because they are not organized. Children are seen working everywhere: serving tea in road side tea stalls working as servants in people's houses.

They are made to work in unhealthy condition. when such children grow up, they feel no sympathy for society. They become ultimately delinquent and engage themselves in violent acts one of the basic requirements for removing child labour is to provide free and compulsory education to all children up to 14 years. If poverty is removed, the need for child labour will automatically decline. Abolition of child labour must be preceded by improving the economic condition of the families concerned. The government of India must ensure that the needs of the poor are fulfilled. In other words, effective abolition of child labour depends on the improvement of the employment opportunities of the adults.

My Ambition in life.

I want to become a doctor. There is every reason behind my choice. Firstly, it is a noble profession. A doctor renders invaluable service to the society. He/she meets patients daily and tries to cure them. sometimes the patients are given a new lease of life. The doctor finds ample satisfaction. A doctor commands a lot of respect from the society. Secondly, ours is a poor country. Most people live in the villages. The basics of health and hygiene are still unknown to them. Ignorance endangers their lives. our children die every day for the wanton lack of minimum medication. I feel for them. I want to reach them. My profession will surely enable me to come in close contact with the suffers. There for I want to be a noble doctor.

Midday meal in school.

The midday meal system is a part of the national programme of nutritional support. It was launched on 15th August, 1995 by the govt. of India. It was made for the children of classes 1-viii of govt. and govt. - aided schools. Most of the children of our country are poor, illiterate and underfed. so the supreme court directed the govt. of India to provide cooked meals to all the children of the country. The midday meal programme aims to improve the health and primary education. Many poor children will come to school in large numbers. It will increase attendance in the school and reduce the dropout rate, only a square meal a day will bring thousands of children to school. They will learn the value of living together.

Terrorism

Terrorism means use of violence and intimidation to achieve a specific purpose. It is one of the serious problems faced by the society today. Individuals or groups resort to violent actions to elicit support from the people. They force the government to yield to their demands. Terrorism is undoubtedly, the worst heinous crime against humanity. Blowing up of planes and railway bridges, explosion of passenger buses, attacking different hotels and resorts are all instances of cruel terrorist activities.

The terrorist organizations like Laskar-e-Taiba, Jaish-e-Mohammad, Al-Quida, Hujietc, have spread their tentacles everywhere. Terrorist activities bring normal life to a standstill. The economy is a country suffers s great setback in the absence peaceful atmosphere.

Global Warming

The unusual rise of average temperature of the earth is called global warming. It is the result of the excessive release of greenhouse gases in the atmosphere. The greenhouse gases are mainly carbon dioxide (CO2), Sulphur dioxide (SO2), Methane (CH4), Nitrous oxide (NO)and water vapours. The amount of these gases in the atmosphere is increasing day by day due to the burning of fossil fuels like coal, petroleum and natural gasses. They act as a blanket and trap the geat released from the earth. so, the average temperature of the earth goes up and causes global warming. It directly leads to climate change of the world. Scientists have already predicted that the average temperature of the earth will rise from 1. 4°Cto5. 8°C by the coming time.

Advertisement

Advertising is a method of conveying a message to the public. In particular,an advertisement seeks to present a positive image of a company, brand,product or service.

Thus,Advertising what we call a brand's communication to the general public. By means of adverts in print media,in video form, and in visual formats like Bill boards, companies can convey the quality of their products.

The intention of advertisement is usually to create demand to make members of the public want to buy a product .often, this is done by showing people how much easier their lives would be if they bought the product. Thus, Advertising to show a product's usefulness.

Advertisement is also to maintain existing demand. As well as creating new customers, adverts try to ensure that existing customers stay interested in the products .Advertisement thus also aims to inspire trust and loyalty.

Adverts often try to capture the sprit of the time .They can be fun and entertaining to watch .But they also have a program magic purpose,to get the general public interested in parting with their money.

GST

Goods and services Tax (GST) refers t to an indirect tax.The implementation of this tax is in India. The collection of this tax takes place from the point of consumption. This is in contrast to collection from the point of origin like previous taxes further more, this tax'simposition is at every step in the production process. The refund is for all the parties in the various stages of production. Also, GST includes almost all indirect taxes .

- Explanation of GST.

First of all, goods and services tax (GST) is a single tax system. The imposition of this tax takes place jointly by the center and the state.further more,the imposition happens with the recomendation of a federal council.

In GST,the goods and services are divided into five different tax slabs.This is for the purpose of the tax collection. Above all, the tax slabsare 0%,5%,12%,18% and 28%also,petroleum products, alcoholic drinks,and electricity do come under GST Rough precious and semi precious stones carry a special rate of 0.25%gold also carries a special rate of 3%.

GSTcertainlysubsumed several taxes and levies.These include central excise duty,services tax,and additional customs duty,furthermore, state level vat,surcharges,and octroi also come under GST.The GSTregime has done away with levies.Also,these levies were applicable to inter state transportation of goods.most note worthy, the application of GST is on all transactions.These transctions are sale,purchase,transfer, lease and import.

- Benefits of GST

First of all, the cascading tax effect refers to a tax on tax.most note worthy, GST eliminates the cascading effects of tax.This is because GST is a comprehensive indirect tax.it certainly brings almost all indirect taxation under one umbrella. Another notable advantage of GST is the increase in the threshold for registration. Earlier a vat was applied if the turn over was more than Rs 5 lakh.This vat'sapplication was upon a business. Further more, there was no service tax when turn over was less than RS10 lakh .In contrast under GSTthis threshold is RS 20 lakh.Hence,this means an exemptions many small traders and service providers.

Unemployment

Unemployment is the inability to get employed in an established organization despite the unsuccessful efforts. It is a persistent condition that cause prolonged starvation in a financially weak family.This problem in the present century has become crucial due to various reasons such as lack of human capital, illiteracy, and availability of resources, crime rate, mental stress,and even the influence of political factors. One of the paramount problems in the working sector is the exploitation of employees, making lose them hope from their work place. They face in equality in the distribution of wages by their employer. More over, favoritism is dominant in work places.The employer'sfavourite and unskilled candidates are preferred more than the skilled ones.

Covid 19

Coronaviruses are a large family of viruses that cause illness ranging from the common cold to more severe diseases such as middle east respiratory syndrome and severe acute respiratory syndrome. A novel cornavirus is a new strain that has not been previously identified in humans. Cornaviruses are zoo notice,meaning they are transmitted between animals and people. Several known cornaviruses are circulating in animals that have not yet infected humans.

Common signs of infection include respiratory symptoms, fever, cough,shortness of breath and breathing difficulties.

I more severe cases, infection can cause pneumonia, severe acute respiratory syndrome, kidney failure and even death.

Standard recomendations to present infection spread include regular hand washing, covering mouth and nose when coughing and sneezing, throughly cooking meat and eggs .Avoid close contact with anyone showing symptoms of respiratory illness duch as coughing and sneezing.

Kannyashree Prakalpa

Kannyashree prakalpa introduced by government of westBengal in 2012 is a unique conditional cash transfer scheme which targets adolescent girls aged 13...19 years and offers a two ..Tire scholarship of an annual RS 500 for continuing education (k1)and a one time payment of 25, 000on completion of 18,conditional upon the girl remaining unmarried and continuing education till that age (k2).The aim of this scheme is two fold.to promote secondary among females and stop marriage of girls before the official age of 18.

As there is strong scientific evidence that female education induces higher levels of income and growth, a number of policy interventions have been introduced in most developing countries in clouding India, to augment enrollment and retention rates,while bridging the gender gap at the same time. How ever, these aim to improve enrollment and retention by offering incentives linked issues like attendance.

After sometime They returned. Both of them were annoyed with their masters.Ramu complained, "why did you waste your time?" You could have phoned to find out whether you were there or not. "Shammu expressed his displeasure in these words .why didn't you tell me before?I would not have come out of my room. "He reported that he was not found in the room.Raghu and Rajheaved a sigh .There was really nothing to chose between the two fools.only God could decide who was the lesser fool?

STORY WRITING

Return Gift

Mr. Aggarwal was a very wealthy businessman. One day he was alone sitting at his dining table. It was his birthday. He heard the footsteps of a man behind the curtains. He knew there was a thief there. "come on! Thank you for coming to my house on my Birthday. I am alone, give me your company. "The thief was starving. He had good food and drinks. Mr. Aggarwal gave him a big purse. it had silver coins. years rolled by. His fortunes changed. Mr. Aggarwal was a very poor man now. His business was ruined. Today aed his 50th birthday. But he had become a pauper now. He was alone reflecting over his good old days.

It was at 9 pm. The bell rang, "who can be at such a time to visit a poor man?" thought Aggarwal. He saw a man in a new suit with a lovely bouquet of red roses. He had many packets of gifts, fruits, sweets and a few bottles. He tried to recognise the man." I'm your old thief. replied the man. With the money, you gave me I did some business. Now I am a rich businessman. "Let's celebrate your birthday. "he said. "it is for you, a little return gift." He gave a bag to Mr. Aggarwal. He opened the bag, it was full of new currency notes.

Honestly pays in the long run.

A woodcutter was chopping down trees on the bank of a river. His hands were so much wet with his sweat that he lost his grip over the axe. It slipped away from his hands and fell down into the river. The poor man couldn't even swim. He thought that his axe was lost forever. He was very sad at his misfortune and started sobbing and weeping. Suddenly there was a flash of light. The god of the Forests appeared before him. The woodcutter explained what had happened. The god consoled him, "Don't you worry. I'll get back your axe for you." Having said these words, he dived into the river. After a few moments, he came out with an axe. It was made of gold. "Is this yours?" he asked. The woodcutter only said "No!" A few seconds later he came out of the river with another axe.

It was made of silver. "No, no, sir, this is not mined," said the woodcutter. He dived again and came out with the third axe. The woodcutter cried loudly looking at the axe "Yes, yes, it's mine—the woodcutter's axe with an iron blade." The god of Forests was impressed with the woodcutter's honesty. "Keep all three of these axes as a present from me." The god uttered these words and disappeared.

Arjuna complished marks man.

The celebrated archer guru Dronacharya thought the royal princes the finer points of archery. one day he wanted to test the archery skill of his pupils. They came to a forest. The guru chose a tree standing in the open. He placed a wooden bird on a bare branch of that tree. The princes were asked to stand200yards away and aim at their target one by one. They were to hit the eye of the bird. Yudhishthira was asked to start the competition. He took his bow and looked at his target. "can you see me?" asked Dronacharya, "yes sir!" replied Yudhishthira. "put down your bow". asked the Guru. The disappointed prince retired from the contest. The same thing happened with all other princes. The same question was asked and all of them gave the same answer.

Alyoshya

The narrator describes Alyosha as the "hero" of The Brothers Karamazov and claims that the book is Alyosha's "biography." A young, handsome man of about twenty, Alyosha is remarkable for his extraordinarily mature religious faith, his selflessness, and his innate love of humankind. Alyosha is naturally good: his love of his fellow human beings is simply a part of his personality, and he rarely has to struggle against temptation or doubt. He spends his energy doing good deeds for his fellow men and trying as honestly as he can to help them become happier and more fulfilled. Alyosha is not judgmental and has an uncanny ability to understand the psychology of others. Despite his infallible goodness and his natural advantages, Alyosha has a gentle, easygoing personality that causes almost everyone who knows him to love him.

At the same time, Alyosha is not naïve or innocent. He understands human evil and the burden of sin, but he practices universal forgiveness. Alyosha's religious faith is the cornerstone of his character. His faith in a loving God, strengthened by his close relationship with the monastic elder Zosima, reinforces his love of mankind and his immense capability to do good. Even when Alyosha experiences doubt, his doubt is always resolved by his commitment to do good. At the end of the novel, Alyosha has become the mature embodiment of Zosima's teachings, and he even helps to guarantee Zosima's legacy by spreading his teachings among the young schoolboys of the town, who adore him.

Alyosha is an unusual main character because he does not initiate much of the main action of the novel. Instead, he tends to react calmly to whatever the other characters are driven by passion. But The Brothers Karamazov is a novel that analyzes various ways of life—the coarse sensualism of Fyodor Pavlovich and the cold scepticism of Ivan both come under scrutiny—and questions each of them sharply. Alyosha's way of life seems superior to that of the other characters. He is the moral centre of the novel because he represents the model of attitude and behaviour that Dostoevsky considers the right one, the one most conducive to human happiness and peace instead of the trauma and conflict that afflict most of the novel's other major characters.

The story of the merchant and the jinn.

There lived a merchant in Basra. He had great wealth and traded extensively. One day he was mounting on his horse journeying to a neighbouring country to collect his due. when he felt hungry, he ate a morsel of bread and a date. Having eaten the date, he threw aside the stone. immediately appeared before him a jinn holding a brown sword in his hand. He threatened to kill the merchant, as the stone of the Daye killed his son. The merchant pleaded that he didn't do it intentionally and he should be pardoned.

The jinn replied that his death was indispensable. Saying this he raised his arm to strike him with the sword. The merchant wept bitterly. Then the merchant said that he had debts to pay, property to settle and say good bye to his wife and children. He bound himself with a vow that he would return to his and he could do what he wanted to do with him. The merchant returned to his town, paid everyone what he owed him and informed his wife and children of the event. On hearing this, all members of the family wept. ultimately, the merchant presented himself before the jinn. The jinn was impressed with his honesty and sincerity. He spared the life of the merchant and liberated him. The jinn also gave a lot of gold and jewels to him in the bargain.

True Friends

Raghu and Raj were two friends and neighbours. Raghu had a servant named Ramu .The name of Raj's servant was shammu. Both the servants were big fools.The two friends debated for hours whose servant was a greater fool. At last, they decided to give them a test to find out who was more foolish.

Next morning all the four gathered at Raja'shouse.Raghu told his servants, "Run back to my house and find out if I am there or not."without wasting even for a second, Ramu rushed home. Then Raj called his servant shammu and said, "Hurry up,Go to your room and find out if you are there or not. "Without eventhinkingfor a moment, shammu ran to his room.

The false Diamonds

There lived a rich man in varanasi .He had only one son who had just tamedten. He had a lot of land and property. He wanted to find out a good adviser for his son before his death. The man must be true and honest.This was what the rich man had thought.oneday he invited all his relatives to a grand feast.He asked each of them if he was a wise and good man.Every relative called himself the,"Wise and best man in the world."Ah!"exclaimed the rich man.He gave a diamond to each of his relatives. But one relative remained silent.The rich man asked what he thought of him as a man. The relative replied, "you are a wise and good man there have been wiser and better men than you."

My first day in the land of lilliputians.

I could hear the noises around me. They were faint human voices. Then I left something moving on my body .it came near my face.He was a tiny little man of 3 inches. He was dressed like a soldier. Forty more followed him.I was amazed to see such tiny men.I couldn't understand what they watched to do with me.Then I felt as if a thousand needles were pricking my body. The little men were shooting arrows at me.Then I lay still without moving. One of the elders, perhaps their leader, stood on a raised platform near me. I indicated for food and water. He seemed to understand me. He sent hundreds of men up to my face. I had my dinner, I went to sleep again. This was my first day among lilliputians.

The story of the fisherman.

There was a poor fisherman. It was his custom to cast his net not more than four times a day. One day when he cast his net soon he found it to be very heavy. He pulled up the netbut was disappointed to find in it.the carcass of amass.Hecast the net second time and this time he found only a large jar full of sand and mud.The third time he got only broken jars and pots. He raised his head towards heaven, and said,"o God,though knoweth that I cast not my net more than four times."with the name of God,he cast the net for the last time.This time he found in it a bottle of brass with a stopper of lead, bearing the seal of Suleman. He rejoiced as he could sell it for ten pieces of gold.He shook the bottle and opened it. Nothing came out of it except cloud of smoke which was condensed into a jinn.The jinn threatened to kill him.The fisherman told the jinn that he had liberated him from the bottle and rescued from the bottom of the seat he jinn was unrelenting. The fisherman then said, "How was thou in this bottle? How can it contain the whole body?"He said that he would never believe it until he saw in it .upon this,the jinn was converted into smoke and then became condensed and entered the bottle little by little. The fisherman hastily sealed the bottle .The jinn tried to escape but invading. "Open to me, I may confer benefits Upton tree," said the jinn.The fisherman replied, "Thou liest than accursed!"And he threw the bottle back deep into the sea.

LETTER WRITING

1. Write a letter to the Head of your institution for a transfer certificate.

To

The principal

D.A.V school.

New Delhi

Dear sir

Subject:- Application for a TC(Transfer Certificate).

With all due respect,

  I request you to make necessary arrangements for the grant of Transfer certificate as my father has been transferred to a different place and I won't be able to continue the studies at the present school.

My last day at school will be 15 Nov, 2018.

I shall be highly obliged to you.

Thanking you!

Yours truly,

Rimpa Das.

2. Write an application to the Head of your institution for a free student ship.

To

The Principal,

D.A.V. School.

Sub - prayer for a full free student ship.

Sir,

I beg to state that I have been reading in your school for the last three years. This year, my younger brother has got himself admitted into the school. On the other hand, my eldest brother is reading in the Dhaka medical college. For this it has become really difficult for my father to defray our educational expenses in these hard days.in fact, he does not have so much of income and savings to pay up our tuition fees regularly and meet our various needs like purchase of books and payment of transport charges.For your kind attention, I would like to tell you that I have been doing quite well in all tests and examinations under your able guidance and care.

I therefore, pray and hope that you would be kind enough to grant me a full free student ship.

I remain

Sir,

Your most obediently pupil

Ramesh Das

Class X

Roll No. 1

3. Write an application to the rationing officer for a duplicate rationing card.

To,

The Rationing officer,

Akhaura,

Agartala,

Sir,

Would like to inform you that unfortunately my rationing I card No ******has been lost 1 December 2020.

I request you, therefore, to issue a Duplicate ration card as early as possible.

Yours faithfully

Madan Dutta.

4. Write an application to the manager BSNLcomplaining about an exceedingly high telephone bill.

To,

The Accounts officer,

Agra Telephone Exchange,

Dear sir,

I have received your bill no.921 dated 4 th March 2008 of our Telephone No.274231.

The bill amount is too high. I presume that due to an over sight this mistake has taken place.

Anyway, I am making payment of the bill but at the same time request you to make enquiry about it and to adjust the excess amount with my next bill.

I do sincerely hope that you will appreciate our position and do the needful at the earliest possible do to.

Thanking you,

Yours faithfully,

Value.

5. Write a letter to the editor of an English newspaper about the nuisance of bursting crackers during festivals particularly during the kalipuja.

To,

The Editor,

The Telegraph,

Kolkata..01.

Sir,

I shall be highly obliged if you kindly allow me a little space in the columns of your highly esteemed daily so that I may ventilate my opinion to draw the attention of the concerned authority about the problem caused by bursting crackers during festivals.

Using crackers has now become to be a fashion in every festival. No festival is left without bursting crackers During immersion ceremony of every puja,specially all through the kalipuja, it has been a part and parcel.The bursting of crackers causes huge inconveniences to both old and the young. The life of peace loving people has become a very much difficult. The students can't concentrate their mind in studies.The patients of cardiac and nerve trouble are the worst suffers.They cannot sleep due to extreme sound at night time.The lack of sleep tells upon their fitness and spirit .Besides it causes different serious diseases like sleeplessness, abnormal blood stress, cardiac disturbance, intellectual imbalance, worrieddebility headache and anxiety even permanent deafness. Sometimes, the fire of crackers cause fatal fire accident that even takes away the life of innocent people. I, as a responsible citizen of this society, inview of all these,think that the time has come for the authority to take critical observe of this evil and take important steps to prohibit the manufacture of crackers to mitigate the suffering of many, otherwise the public grievance may at any time, lead to a dire consequence.

Thanking you,
Yours faithfully,
Sangeeta Mondal.
Dated
27th April 2013
Nadia, Nrisingha pur.

6. Write a letter to the editor of an English newspaper about the harm that is caused to the environment by the use of plastic bags and plastic cups.

To,

The Editor,

The English express

Dated 6.04.21

Respected sir,

Through a column in your esteemed daily, I would like to express my views on the major problem of pollution caused by plastic bags and cups in the world we live in. Plastic plays a very important role in making our lives easier. But it has a very negative impact on the earth &the environment around us. Plastic is not disposed &decomposed which has various affects. People use plastic in their day to day lives &throwing here &there which is causing harm to marine animals as well as other animals. Burning plastic causes smoke which adds to the pollution. Innocent animals accidentally eat the animals and die out of choking or by the plastic that becomes poison bait cannot be digested.more over plastic gets logged in the drainage system causing the water to overflow &lead to pollution &dirtyness .Thus we should limit to the use of plastic &use &throw it in a proper way.There fore I request you to print my letter to spread awareness.

Looking forward to your kind help and active co operation.

Yours faithfully,

Ramesh.

7. Write a letter to the editor of an English newspaper expressing your concern about the hardship caused by the continuous rise in the prices of essential articles in cluding medicines.

To
The Editor,
The Hindustan Times,
New Delhi
June 29th, 2021
Sub....High price rise of essential commodities.

Respected sir,

Through the columns of your esteemed newspaper, I would like to draw the attention of the government towards the rising prices of essential commodities.

The problem of rising prises of essential commodities.

The problem of rising prices has become very common .The prices of essential commodities such as pulses,cereals,oil,spices, sugar,onions,medicines,vegetables and other basic necessities of life have touched new heights .The steep rise of prices has hit hard the poor and lower middle class families. It has become very difficult for the people to make both ends meet.The middle class salaried people can't manage their household budgets within their salaries .The poor section of the society and the wage earners are the worst affected. The main reasons of price hike are black marketing, hoarding, fall of production, improper system of distribution and corruption at all levels.

It is high time that governments took necessary steps to control the prices.The government needs to act strictly against the hoarding, blackmarketing and profiteering of essential items. Acts of corruption and bribery must be rooted out.only then the common man can be relieved from the effects of price rise.

Kindly publish my views in your newspaper.

Thanking you,
Yours truely
Gopal

8. Write an application to the manager BSNLcomplaining about an exceedingly high telephone bill.

To,

The Accounts officer,

Agra Telephone Exchange,

Dear sir,

I have received your bill no.921 dated 4 th March 2008 of our Telephone No.274231.

The bill amount is too high. I presume that due to an over sight this mistake has taken place.

Anyway, I am making payment of the bill but at the same time request you to make enquiry about it and to adjust the excess amount with my next bill.

I do sincerely hope that you will appreciate our position and do the needful at the earliest possible do to.

Thanking you,

Yours faithfully,

Value.

9. Write a letter to the editor of an English newspaper about the nuisance of bursting crackers during festivals particularly during the kalipuja.

To,
The Editor,
The Telegraph,
Kolkata..01.

Sir,

 I shall be highly obliged if you kindly allow me a little space in the columns of your highly esteemed daily so that I may ventilate my opinion to draw the attention of the concerned authority about the problem caused by bursting crackers during festivals.

 Using crackers has now become to be a fashion in every festival. No festival is left without bursting crackers During immersion ceremony of every puja,specially all through the kalipuja, it has been a part and parcel.The bursting of crackers causes huge inconveniences to both old and the young. The life of peace loving people has become a very much difficult. The students can't concentrate their mind in studies.The patients of cardiac and nerve trouble are the worst suffers.They cannot sleep due to extreme sound at night time.The lack of sleep tells upon their fitness and spirit .Besides it causes different serious diseases like sleeplessness, abnormal blood stress, cardiac disturbance, intellectual imbalance, worrieddebility headache and anxiety even permanent deafness. Sometimes, the fire of crackers cause fatal fire accident that even takes away the life of innocent people. I, as a responsible citizen of this society, inview of all these,think that the time has come for the authority to take critical observe of this evil and take important steps to prohibit the manufacture of crackers to mitigate the suffering of many, otherwise the public grievance may at any time, lead to a dire consequence.

Thanking you,
Yours faithfully,
Sangeeta Mondal.
Dated
27th April 2013
Nadia, Nrisingha pur.

10. Write a letter to the editor of an English newspaper about the harm that is caused to the environment by the use of plastic bags and plastic cups.

To,

The Editor,

The English express

Dated 6.04.21

Respected sir,

  Through a column in your esteemed daily, I would like to express my views on the major problem of pollution caused by plastic bags and cups in the world we live in. Plastic plays a very important role in making our lives easier. But it has a very negative impact on the earth &the environment around us. Plastic is not disposed &decomposed which has various affects. People use plastic in their day to day lives &throwing here &there which is causing harm to marine animals as well as other animals. Burning plastic causes smoke which adds to the pollution. Innocent animals accidentally eat the animals and die out of choking or by the plastic that becomes poison bait cannot be digested.more over plastic gets logged in the drainage system causing the water to overflow &lead to pollution &dirtyness .Thus we should limit to the use of plastic &use &throw it in a proper way.There fore I request you to print my letter to spread awareness.

  Looking forward to your kind help and active co operation.

Yours faithfully,

Ramesh.

11. Write a letter to the editor of an English newspaper expressing your concern about the hardship caused by the continuous rise in the prices of essential articles in cluding medicines.

To
The Editor,
The Hindustan Times,
New Delhi
June 29th, 2021
Sub....High price rise of essential commodities.

Respected sir,

Through the columns of your esteemed newspaper, I would like to draw the attention of the government towards the rising prices of essential commodities.

The problem of rising prises of essential commodities.

The problem of rising prices has become very common .The prices of essential commodities such as pulses, cereals, oil, spices, sugar, onions, medicines,vegetables and other basic necessities of life have touched new heights. The steep rise of prices has hit hard the poor and lower middle class families. It has become very difficult for the people to make both ends meet.The middle class salaried people can't manage their household budgets within their salaries .The poor section of the society and the wage earners are the worst affected. The main reasons of price hike are black marketing, hoarding, fall of production, improper system of distribution and corruption at all levels.

It is high time that governments took necessary steps to control the prices.The government needs to act strictly against the hoarding, blackmarketing and profiteering of essential items. Acts of corruption and bribery must be rooted out.only then the common man can be relieved from the effects of price rise.

Kindly publish my views in your newspaper.

Thanking you,
Yours truely
Gopal

12. Write a letter to the principal about an application for school leaving certificate.

To,

The principal,

D.A.V public school,

Ranchi.

Dated 1st January.

Sub Application of school leaving certificate.

Respected sir,

With due respect, I would like to state that my father has been transferred to Bokaro.He has to join there for his job within 10 days.We are going to shift the coming Sunday, ie.15th of the month.Therefore, I request you to kindly issue me my school transfer certificate, so that I would be able to join a school there.I have cleared all my pending dues and returned all the library books.

Thanking you.

Yours sincerely,

Raju pal.

13. Write a letter to the transport officer a problem with the transportation system your area.

Dear sir,

I am writing this letter to inform you about the transport system, which is causing a lot of in convenience to the people. There are various problems people faced due to the inconvenience by the public bus service. As bus does not reach the bus stand on time. The buses are in poor condition and misbehavior of bus conductor is a major concern.

As buses are always delayed professionals are not able to reach offices on time.secondly, the busesare in very bad condition to extant that windows are broken &there is no sign of cleanliness.

More over, the bus conductor does not behave well as there has been a fight with passengers many times.

I suggest if some changes are implemented, it can solve all the problems that people are experiencing. Firstly, the bus driver should be strictly informed to reach the   bus station   on time .secondly, The issue regarding keeping the bus clean can be resolved by appointing the sweepers.

Lastly, the bus conductor should be strictly advised not to indulge in the fight with passengers.

I hope you will take some strict action.

Yours faithfully,

Mandeep Singh.

14. Write a letter to the editor of an English newspaper about the problem caused by bursting crackers during festivals.

To,
The Editor,
The Telegraph,
Kolkata...01.
Sir,

I shall be highly obliged if you kindly allow me a little space in the columns of your highly esteemed daily so that I may ventilate my opinion to draw the attention of the concerned authority about the problem caused by bursting crackers during festivals. Using crackers has now become to be a fashion in every festival. No festival is left without bursting crackers. During immersion ceremony of every puja, specially all through the kalipuja, it has been a part and parcel.The bursting of crackers causes huge inconveniences to both old and the young. The life of peace loving people has become a very much difficult. The students can't concentrate their mind in stdies. The patients of cardiac and nerve trouble are the worst suffers.

They can't sleep due to extreme sound at night time.The lack of sleep tells upon their fitness and spirit .Besides it causes different serious diseases like sleeplessness, a normal blood stress, cardiac disturbance, intellectual imbalance, worried debility, headache and anxiety even permanent deafness. Sometimes the fire of crackers cause fatal fire accident that even takes away the life of innocent people.

I, as a responsible citizen of this society, in view of all these, think that the time had come for the authority to take critical observe of this evil and take important steps to prohibit the manufacture of crackers to mitigate the suffering of many, otherwise the public grievance may, at any time, lead to a dire consequence.

Thanking you,
Yours faithfully, Sangeeta Mondal.

15. Write a letter to the editor of a newspaper commenting on reckless driving.

To,

The Editor,

The states man,

Kolkata.. 01

Sir,

Subject..Expressing concern over reckless driving.

Through the column of your seemed newspaper, I wish to draw the kind attention of the concerned authorities and the general public towards the issue of more and more cases of reckless driving everyday. Accidents due to reckless driving are the order of the day. The speed maniacs responsible for the most of the Accidents disappear from the scene leaving it the victims bleeding and crying. After knocking down a person, they flee before anybody can note down the number of their vehicles.They have no humidity left in them they think that the road is their private property. Reckless drivers overtake from the leftdis regarding all traffic rules.

Traffic lights no meaning for them. The penalties imposed for reckless driving are too lenient to be effective. Time is ripe to impose heavy penalties on offenders. A reckless driver who speeds away after knocking down a person should be forced to spend at least one year in the prison cell,after being caught by the police. I shall be really obliged to you for your kind consideration of providing a relevant space to my views in your esteemed daily.

Yours sincerely

Rama kanta.